# THE
# SMARTEST BOOK
# IN THE WORLD

*A Lexicon of Literacy, A Rancorous Reportage,*
*A Concise Curriculum of Cool*

## GREG PROOPS

Illustrations by Jennifer Canaga

TOUCHSTONE
New York   London   Toronto   Sydney   New Delhi

TOUCHSTONE
An Imprint of Simon & Schuster, Inc.
1230 Avenue of the Americas
New York, NY 10020

First Touchstone hardcover edition May 2015

TOUCHSTONE and colophon are registered trademarks of Simon & Schuster, Inc.

For information about special discounts for bulk purchases,
please contact Simon & Schuster Special Sales at 1-866-506-1949
or business@simonandschuster.com.

The Simon & Schuster Speakers Bureau can bring authors to your live event. For more
information or to book an event, contact the Simon & Schuster Speakers Bureau at
1-866-248-3049 or visit our website at www.simonspeakers.com.

Manufactured in the United States of America

1    3    5    7    9    10    8    6    4    2

Library of Congress Cataloging-in-Publication Data

Proops, Greg.
The smartest book in the world : a lexicon of literacy, a rancorous
reportage, a concise curriculum of cool / Greg Proops ;
illustrations by Jennifer Canaga.—First Touchstone hardcover edition.
    pages cm
    1.  American wit and humor.  I. Title.
    PN6165.P76 2015
    818'.602—dc23
                        2014038428

ISBN 978-1-4767-4704-0
ISBN 978-1-4767-4706-4 (ebook)

*For Jennifer*

# INTRODUCTION

Hurray, hurrah, you made it to *The Smartest Book in the World*. You are now officially more inquisitive than all your bored friends. In your hands you hold a clamorous compendium, a rancorous reportage, a lexicon of literacy. This is the burning bush, the Rosetta stone, the Fountain of Youth, the Grail to all the funnest knowledge and most freaktastical answers to the questions you've never asked, like: *Which Roman emperor would be the best first baseman?* and *Does vodka go with vodka?* You know, the vitals.

Lots of comedians write first-person memoirs of their hilarious experiences in show business. This is not a bad thing. We like to see comedians get work. Sometimes they tell stories about their dog or people they shagged. This book is not one of those. I don't have a dog. The people I know don't have dog stories, either. Not even shaggy ones. To be sure, the experiences are there, but this round it's better to mine the vast worlds outside one's career and troll for laughs and the occasional fact.

What makes you so smart? I hear you ask. Stop sniveling. It does not happen overnight. One must spend years traveling, studying, and performing to rapt, attentive, worshipful crowds. Since that was practically impossible, I self-anointed and did a Proopcast. The knowledge collected is for us to share. You will be excited, then ashamed, then inflamed, then engaged.

Thank you for buying this. If you stole it, well done, you. You are going to make your way in this world. If you borrowed it, return it full. Let us take to the ether.

# THE PROOPS COMMANDMENTS

## 1. THERE WILL BE ANCIENT HISTORY

> The past is never dead. It's not even past.
> —William Faulkner

> Yet is it more honorable, and just, and upright, and pleasing,
> to treasure in the memory good acts than bad.
> —Xenophon, *Anabasis*

I am aware that just saying "ancient history" makes you fidget in your seat and look at the clock. I feel you. But these aren't just dinky people wearing togas and writing out love notes on papyrus. We are talking about the most violent, sexually aberrant, mentally unstable people in the history of our blue planet. And those were just the leaders. Every form of vice and villainy was practiced: gluttony, lust, genocide, patricide, infanticide, regicide, usury, perversion, treachery, and always lots of awesome slavery. Their fighting and boinking would make a Led Zeppelin after party look like playschool. We are going to throw down on the ancient groove monkeys of the past who changed the funk for all times.

Just sneak a peek at Nero, the Roman emperor and famous maniac, who prowled the streets at night mugging people and molesting Women with his pals. The louche emperor even took up acting and had a group of guys applaud for him at festivals. He also married two men and had one castrated so he could be his "wife." And for his final act of depravity, he stomped his pregnant wife to death. Then we have the emperor Tiberius, who left his job and moved to the Isle of Capri just to perv it up. He had a pool full of boys who would swim up to him and nibble at his imperial giblets; they were called "minnows." Feeling queasy? Try this fine lady, Julia the daughter of Emperor Augustus, who used to take on all comers late at night right in the Forum. You get the mosaic. For the hat trick, we have Cleopatra, who had a pleasure barge with purple sails and perfumed dancing girls, so put down your smartphone and reconsider the past.

While bringing debauchery to new heights in the three centuries from Alexander the Great to Cleopatra, the world also perfected medicine, theater, wine, philosophy, logic, Christianity, democracy, the written word, the zero, astronomy, bronze, the Olympics, falafel, gladiator sandals, and, perhaps most importantly, the sports stadium with vendors, beer, bleachers, sun roofs, and a luxury box. The Colosseum in Rome had a retractable sunroof made of sails that was manned by a local unit of sailors. The tickets to amphitheaters were perforated and stamped so one could tell which section to sit in and attendance could be accurately counted. Alexander brought engineers who measured the distance they traveled in conquering the world. The steam engine and the computer were invented but discarded because slave labor made them redundant. Yet we destroy the sites of their glory willy-nilly and pay no heed to their warnings and wisdom. We of this age have bombed and made war on ancient Babylon, Parthia, Mesopotamia, and the timeless city of Damascus. The very places where civilization was invented and the Bible took place. The ancients advised love is the joy of the good, the wonder of the wise, the amazement of the gods. Tough lesson, that one.

I'm not here to sound like the *Antiques Historical Roadshow.* The old days were rarely the *good* old days; they were damn fine for a few people with eunuchs, a personal army, and a villa. For most others, they were lucky not to end up being a chariot speed bump. It was a good day if you could avoid bristling arrows, marauding armies, raging phalanxes, or boiling oil. To make no mention of the epidemics, floods, and occasional rains of frogs for a change of plague.

But for pure flash, the ancients knew how to party with prostitutes of dazzling variety and proclivity, build colossal monuments and temples of marble, paint statues, and had the know-how to roast an ox with a goose in it (take that, turducken). I'm not saying we should go back to the age of enslavement, but we could use a dash of that faith and single-mindedness that it took to build aqueducts and pyramids and the like. Our current defining philosophy is one of raw self-interest. Was it always thus? Yes, but with an explanation. People then conquered the world astride a white horse wearing a plumed helmet, the troops singing, flutes playing in the dusty breeze. Today the conquerors meet in a climate-controlled conference room in Switzerland and lack all of that bravura. Alexander claimed he was the son of Zeus. Those who run the world now have no such distinction of lineage. Alexander read Homer. There is no poetry in leadership now because it's not printed on money. And in all that time, nobody ever texted a picture of their genitalia—they cast it in bronze and hung it as a lucky oil lamp.

## 2. THERE WILL BE MOVIES

The *Smartest Book* has a no-3-D policy, but the movies here are not necessarily the critical darlings of all time; some are just plain fun. But even fun requires craft and respect for the audience. These movies respect you and invite you to live in their world. These pictures are the funnest and goodest. They are what you need right now. If you have seen them—good for you, time to revisit. If not, get watching; life is too short to spend any more time on *Iron Man 9* or *The Hangover 6*. The films here will divert you, some may even move you. Thrill to the booming monument that is Anita Ekberg in a fountain in *La Dolce Vita*, taste the wild screaming estrogen flow in the semidocumentary music-video style of Richard Lester letting the Beatles loose in *A Hard Day's Night*, take back the night with truck-shooting, convenience-store-robbing badasses Susan Sarandon and Geena Davis in *Thelma & Louise*. Take a long look and appreciate the actors who are Movie Helpers, actors who make any movie they are in more entertaining no matter how dreary, like quirky Hebrew sex symbol Jeff Goldblum in *Igby*, who always appears to be in a different, better, funnier, quirkier movie than whatever movie he is actually appearing in, especially when he is in a *Jurassic Park* sequel. The bombshells get a workout by dropping the fire on your libido; that's right, Rita Hayworth in *Gilda* is made of solid chrome hot. The earthy Scandinavian lava pool Ingrid Bergman in *Casablanca* is a dame so smoking she makes you join a band of rebels. Tallulah Bankhead brings bisexuality to gravel-voiced, dizzying heights in *Lifeboat*. If movies aren't better than life, then why live?

## 3. THERE WILL BE SATCHEL PAIGE

Ain't no man can avoid being born average,
but there ain't no man got to be common.
—Satchel Paige

Satchel Paige was an all-star ace pitcher, up and down North, South, East, and West America. He played for countless teams and was a veteran of thousands of baseball games and a million miles on the road. He didn't always show up on time, and in general, rules did not apply to him. His stories are to be taken with a grain of showbiz, but that is what elevates him above other baseball greats. The man had super charisma and blarney. He is ageless, immortal, a clown, a showman, a barnstormer, a teller of tall tales, a ghetto success story, a civil rights pioneer, a black superstar. He hung with Jelly Roll Morton, played the guitar, blew through loads of money, wore flashy suits with gaudy ties, married at least three women, collected antiques, showed up in a cowboy movie with Robert Mitchum, told big stories, misremembered superstars' names, and held court for generations. Facts were never set in stone for Paige. His name isn't even Paige. His family changed it from Page to class things up. His date of birth is movable. He was a sage and a teacher; life was his subject, baseball was the school. Class commences now.

## 4. THERE WILL BE POETRY

> When power leads man towards arrogance, poetry reminds him of his limitations. When power narrows the areas of man's concern, poetry reminds him of the richness and diversity of his existence. When power corrupts, poetry cleanses. For art establishes the basic human truths which must serve as the touchstones of our judgment.
> —John F. Kennedy

> Poetry is the shortest distance between two humans.
> —Lawrence Ferlinghetti

Poetry gets a bad rap. In Ireland, poets are venerated. In America, poetry is scary if it don't rhyme. Schools don't teach students to seek out the poetry in life; rather, they are taught to conform and fit into boxes. Poetry is a rebellion. These poets spoke of love, to be certain, but there is revolution in the verse. Baudelaire scandalized Paris. Poe frightens generations. Villon had to run for his life. Ovid was banned from Rome. Poetry is the shield. Poetry is the key to the other world where we all belong. These poems and these poets are outcasts and outlaws, outsiders, visionaries, and outliers.

Poetry is included here because life is an endless series of narrow-minded oyster heads trying to revoke you. It's an arid desert devoid of humanity. It's a horrid poisonous rainfall of shards of obsidian smashing down upon your heart; it's hideous career choices that you regret the rest of your life; it's relationships you enter into with every bloody possibility of failure at the outset, and yet you dash into them like a heedless albino bat through a cave as swiftly as you can to your own inevitable demise against a sticky-ass stalagmite where they find you, centuries later, struggling in your death throes, that's why. Poetry helps alleviate that. We live in a world where Dick Cheney gets to walk around and do whatever he wants; Vladimir Putin is in charge of a country, though he is clearly a certifiable maniac; and Donald Trump is invited to share his thoughts. That is why we need poetry. Light some incense, pour yourself a chalice of elderberry wine, and slide down into a comfy chair. It won't be as bad as you think.

## 5. THERE WILL BE MUSIC

Music is a moral law. It gives soul to the universe, wings to the mind, flight to the imagination, and charm and gaiety to life and to everything.
—Plato

The Smartest Book admits that music is subjective. Some people, as Donny and Marie once so sagely observed, are a little bit country, some a little bit rock 'n' roll. One thing is certain: there is no accounting for taste. If there were, why would Sting and the Police have enjoyed such an enduring career? His name is Sting; aren't you embarrassed? If rock is supposed to be cool and represent rebellious rockers snorting drugs and blazing on bitchin' motorcycles, what would be the uncoolest name for a band ever? Let us conclude, the Police. Why not call yourselves the Federal Bureau of Bummer?

Music is food for the soul and snacks for the shallow good times. Therefore, you must have music for every state of mind and emotion. These are albums you must have for the sake of your own musical life. No Journey, Black Eyed Peas, Foreigner, Kiss, Miley, Justin Bieber, no stadium white-guy gimme-cap rock or any junk where Auto-Tuning is used. Those albums are evil and only a clam head who has lost their ability to discern the singing of angels from the brainless bleetings of a toaster oven could enjoy them. From the grumpy confines of the fortress of Proopitude, thus have we spoken.

## 6. THERE WILL BE NO WHINING

There will be occasional boring preachy parts, but you are expected to act like a grown-up and eat your spinach. It's good for you, goddammit. Get some fortitude and fiber into your diet. Grow a pair of female members. You are not required to agree with everything you read. That is submission. But laughing at it and trying to understand something you do not concur with is called being sophisticated.

It is entirely your prerogative to agree or disagree with my assertions. But consider this: you may not have spent as many hours riding in a bus across the Saskatchewan prairie contemplating the vast contributions of Canadian rock musicians or hung out at a roadside truck stop in Turkey deconstructing an old *Kojak* episode. If you are the kind of person who says they think they read something somewhere, let this be the place you read it and maybe remember. Retention is not required; I will always be right here and right, here.

## 7. THERE WILL BE ART

If you want to really hurt your parents, and you don't have the
nerve to be gay, the least you can do is go into the arts.
—Kurt Vonnegut, *A Man Without a Country*

Art is as essential as air to a mammal, as sun to a reptile, as sup-
pression to a bureaucrat, as a metaphor to a writer grappling for
examples. Art exists so we can rise out of the filth of chasing
money and doing our corporate masters' bidding. Art doesn't
change the world; art is the bloody world. Let's then try to take it
from where the rich elite keep it in a museum. We will see if we
can extricate art from its exclusive stronghold and put it back in
your crib. Please do not actually try to steal art or break the law in
any way. We cannot be responsible for how easily swayed you are
and how little willpower you possess. So don't even think about
it. Unless your plan is foolproof, then meet me in the car park and
look for the black van with the rearing horse airbrushed on the
side. We will answer to "Miguel."

## 8. WE WILL SPELL *WOMAN*
## WITH A CAPITAL *W*

There is a movement by all the men in the world to make sure
Women don't get a fair shake. Men yell at Women from cars. Men
deny Women equal pay. Men tell Women to "smile." Men off their
wives and girlfriends. Men enact laws to keep Women from health
care they need. This is not opinion, this is fact. The reason is a
Woman dreamed the universe into existence. Women give birth,
men take life. Therefore, men are jealous of this power. War is men-
struation envy. A Woman dreamed the universe into being. That is
why it is called "the Big Bang"—only a Woman can make a bang

that big. If a man had done it, it would be called the Disappointingly Early Theory of the Universe. Men can only give birth to sacred bullets through their Viagra-assisted manshaft. Women deal with the pain of childbirth; men act like they have diphtheria if they get a cold. We all know Columbus and George Washington, but who is taught about Sojourner Truth or Susan B. Anthony? Women in the United States could not vote until 1920. Then only because they demanded it for years. Any advances Women have made they have done by organizing and being better at everything than men just to be recognized and heard. They have to.

A few things to ponder as you seek to improve and enlighten yourself out of the depths of your ignorance:

- Germany, New Zealand, Argentina, India, Chile, Brazil, Pakistan, the UK, Ireland, Canada, and Australia, to name but a few, have had Women leaders. The USA has not.
- Women, as of right now, dominate publishing. J. K. Rowling is the most-read author on Earth.
- Understand telling a Woman to "smile" is an imposition and a demand you have no right to make.
- Don't use the term "old lady" as a pejorative term. Old Women raise the world and know everything. They are anything but weak.
- When you go into a bar or restaurant, notice if the Woman servers are made to wear hot outfits. Consider which places make men do that.
- Victoria's Secret has a TV special. Calvin Klein's men's undies do not.
- Women are the majority of workers in the world. They do not get equal pay, and they have to put up with men's shit attitude, groping, and harassment.
- Women are regularly assaulted, raped, beaten, abused, murdered, sold, and disappeared. Everywhere. That means in America as well. This is not the top story in the news. Ever.

Therefore, Women get a big *W*, and you will have to wait to be heard for once, dude.

## 9. THERE WILL BE WORDS

Words make sentences make sense. Words can illuminate and illustrate, denigrate and castigate. Words come easy to some, to others—including a certain president of the United States, who had a deuce of a time pronouncing *nuclear* without putting the *nuke* before the *culer*—they remain "deciders." Some people enjoy great facility with words, others stumble over the simplest thoughts. Have you ever heard your uncle attempt to tell a coherent joke? Time to crack open the lexicon and let the thrills begin. You will quiver incandescently at the new breadth of expression you will attain. With little strenuous exertion on your behalf, you will find your corpus awash in expressions, redolent with remarks, conflated with commands, filled with phrases, and ready to take on that dinner party with those complete ninnies whose very presence makes your stomach churn. Improve your life all around by worshiping the flame that words ignite. You will be dazzled, pyrolatrous.

## 10. THERE WILL BE BOOKS

> Do not read, as children do, to amuse yourself, or like the ambitious, for the purpose of instruction. No, read in order to live.
> —Gustave Flaubert

And more books. Reading stretches the imagination. Books are better than movies, and movies are better than life, so therefore, books are better than life. Books have a bad rep as being too time-consuming. "I am too busy to read," you hear. "I have to buy some quinoa, then take the twins to their postnatal yoga class, then update my Facebook page, then make a gluten-free pizzetta from scratch." You do have time, you are just too determined to be uninformed. Life is confusing and unclear, books are amusing and, at worst, thought-provoking. No book ever asks for the rent or threatens you with a knife. No book ever borrows money or agrees to help you to move and then is too hungover to show up. Books are the cheapest, most readily available, easiest to carry, best way on Earth to keep your mind racing, your heart thumping, and your sense of adventure piqued. Crack one open with me and let's get drunk on text. We will put the *text* back in *texting* and the *context* back in *context*.

## 11. THERE WILL BE GOOD DRUGS
## AND GOOD TIMES

Light one up or pour one down, and let's all get together and put on wings like Icarus and see how high we can go tonight before the horrible flaming demon sun that the Man made out of his hideous nuclear agenda burns our delicate artistic wings and sends our sensitive behinds spiraling back to the ground like a burnt McNugget full of regret. Or let's just horse around until something funny happens. And if you are clean and sober, hooray for you. Be a lamb chop and go get the corkscrew—oh, and refill the ice bucket as well, will you, darling? You can drive everyone home later.

# THE PROOPTIONARY I

LANGUAGE, n. the music with which we charm
the serpents guarding another's treasure.
—Ambrose Bierce, *The Devil's Dictionary*

Words is all we gots. We bend them, parse them, define and redefine them, twist and twirl them, ignore, abuse, and mispronounce them. People who aren't listened to shout them. Books are chock-full of them. Learn some new ones here and reset some old ones. People will be amazed and delighted with your supes new vocab or ignore you and go back to their phones and virtual obligations. Either way you win. A secret win is the best kind of win because only you have to celebrate. Word. The Prooptionary is mercifully short and calibrated with your busy schedule in mind. All work and no play, as they say. These are in Proopabetical order.

> Proopabetical order is the order of a river flowing upstream, a waft of smoke from a lit reefer, the condensation running down the frosty side of an icy cold vodka-flavored vodka drink. Chaos theory holds that a small deviation in a set of systems creates unpredictable results. Proopabetical order exists only as long as the outsider is reading it but wonders where that leaves you.

**Whatnot (n.):** Sometimes defined as something trivial or indefinite. This totally underestimates the importance of trivia. One person's trivia is another person's reason for living. For instance, one may know little about life, as it is full of bank notices and insurance bills that signify nothing. But one can fill up on trivia about, say, old-time baseball. While that may not make pragmatic day-to-day living easier, it is a cozy bolt hole to run to when the world seems too present. As for indefiniteness, no one word encapsulates our experience on this green swinging sphere as much as *indefinite*. So take that, *trivia*. Also the *Oxford English Dictionary* defines *whatnot* as: a stand with shelves for small objects. No one has ever used that definition of whatnot from your bloody book and whatnot.

In a sentence:

"The room was douchily flooded with hipsters and tattooed hat wearers and *whatnot*."

**Fantastic (adj.):** This serves as the most versatile of adjectives. Yes, it means fanciful and whatnot. But it also means *wonderful* and *terrific*, isn't that fantastic? *Fantastic* can mean strange, imaginary, made up, or just huge. That is the versatility we are looking for. From the Greek *phantastikos*: able to imagine images in your mind. That is super fantastic.

In a sentence:

"Let's get live, catch some toast, and hit that pie place."
"*Fantastic.*"
"Those are some *fantastic* slingbacks you are wearing, pumpkin butter."
"*Fantastic* of you to say so, love shack."

**Swerve (int.):** This is not about turning sharply to avoid hitting something or whatever the *OED* says that is so obvious. You may say "swerve" to someone you wish to avoid or to dismiss an inopportune request. But the meaning we propose is to party in a fulfilling way. A swerve, like a good mood, is something that must be put on. One gets one's own swerve on.

In a sentence:

"Hey, wanna come to my party?"
"*Swerve.*"

"Give me a cigarette."

*"Swerve."*

"Babycake, hand me the vaporizer. I gots to get my *swerve* on."

**Adore (v.):** super-happening verb. Better than *like*. More sophisticated than *nuts about* or *wet for*. *Adore* makes life more like a madcap black-and-white picture from the '30s where people wear evening clothes and drink gimlets and have drivers in giant open-air sedans.

In a sentence:

"Hey, big boy, more mustard on your hot dog?"

"I would simply *adore* a tad more, you minx."

**Possum (adv.):** possibly. Maybe. Might could. Like a nocturnal marsupial.

In a sentence:

"Could you *possum* answer the door?"

"It's a *possum* with ability."

**Incontestable/ly (adj./adv.):** No argument, you must use this whenever anyone questions even the slightest measure of taste in your presence. It is these kinds of bon mots that will get you invited to many sexy dinner parties with decent wine and a balcony to smoke on.

In a sentence:

"This is *incontestably* the most desperately dire spinach salad in the long-storied history of humankind."

"The hideousness of that pinhead's gimme cap is *incontestable*."

**Kleptocracy (n.):** In the United States, what we used to call democracy. It means the government is run by thieves. If you don't not believe the United States is a kleptocracy, then you are a Pollyanna. You must now go look up *Pollyanna* on your own.

In a sentence:

"Good morning, Mr. President, that is a fantastically big *kleptocracy* you have got there."

"Thank you, Mr. Prime Minister, the *kleptocracy* I preside over is adored by the wealthy."

**Pollyanna (n.):** (Here it is. You shouldn't have to wait.) Annoyingly optimistic in the face of reality.

In a sentence:

"The dictionary indicates that *Pollyanna* rhymes with French Guiana. That would give even a depressed rhymer the blind optimism of a *Pollyanna* that you would be required to rhyme French Guiana with anything."

"I never wanna hear from any cheerful *Pollyannas*/Who tell you fate supplies a mate—it's all bananas."

—"But Not for Me," George and Ira Gershwin

**Bon mot (n.):** a witty remark. Time to add some French to your game, *n'est-ce pas*? Spend all your time thinking of these and then crack them out when the chips are down. Laughter almost always wins the day and can undo many awkward situations. Only a smart-ass calls a joke a bon mot. Dorothy Parker, who was wit personified, declared, "Wit has truth in it; wise-cracking is simply calisthenics with words." She also quipped, "One more drink and I'd have been under the host." That is wit. Try it. It is refreshing, like being happy for a friend.

In a sentence:

"Gwyneth Paltrow is a food blogger like someone on death row is a life coach."

"What an incontestably rich *bon mot*, you rapscallion."

**Plutocracy (n.):** a country that is ruled by the richest people. The most accurate word currently in our possession.

Thomas Jefferson on plutocracy: "The end of democracy and the defeat of the American Revolution will occur when government falls into the hands of lending institutions and moneyed incorporations."

In a sentence:

"But we're not a democracy. It's a terrible misunderstanding and a slander to the idea of democracy to call us that. In reality, we're a *plutocracy*: a government by the wealthy."

—Ramsey Clark, former U.S. Attorney General

**Oligarchy (n.):** a government in which a small group exercises control, especially for corrupt and selfish purposes. This could never happen. Go back to sleep.

In a sentence:

"Monarchy degenerates into tyranny, aristocracy into *oligarchy*, and democracy into savage violence and chaos."

—Polybius

**Cat (n.):** No, not the one with four paws. Picture Miles Davis. Now picture him walking away from you. That's one mean cat.

In a sentence:

"Man, that *cat* [Ornette Coleman] is nuts."

—Thelonious Monk

**Feminist (n.):** A misunderstood word, *feminism* is simply the idea that men and Women are equal and should be treated as equals. For some men, this is truly terrifying, like being disagreed with or told no. There exists a male rights movement. This is a nonstarter. Men have all the rights. Somebody needs to learn to share.

In a sentence:

"People call me a *feminist* whenever I express sentiments that differentiate me from a doormat or a prostitute."

—Rebecca West

**Freedom (n.):** the power or right to act, speak, or think as one wants without hindrance or restraint. This term is overused by people who do not believe in it; it is rarely practiced in real life. Freedom is quite subjective; most people find it a bit too much responsibility. Governments and large institutions like to put parameters on it so everyone will feel comfortable with not having to think for themselves.

From Ambrose Bierce's *The Devil's Dictionary* on freedom: "A political condition that every nation supposes itself to enjoy in virtual monopoly. Liberty: The distinction between *freedom* and *liberty* is not accurately known; naturalists have never been able to find a living specimen of either."

In a sentence:

"*Freedom* is the *freedom* to say that two plus two make four. If that is granted, all else follows."

—George Orwell, *1984*

---

Ambrose Bierce was a cynic, a poet, disgruntled husband, tragic father, war hero, and intrepid journalist. He loathed demagoguery and puffery and was quite capable and savage with a pen. He served in the Civil War, saw action at Shiloh and Chickamauga, and wrote the horrifying and evocative short story "An Occurrence at Owl Creek Bridge." Kurt Vonnegut said he thought it was the greatest American short story. Bierce fought in the Civil War and fought against corruption as a journalist in San Francisco. At seventy-one, he purportedly disappeared while following the bandit revolutionary Pancho Villa in Mexico and was never seen again. So your story about how you took a bike trip to the Poconos isn't cutting it. Bierce's is an astounding writing life. *The Devil's Dictionary* is his compendium of vitriol. Something he made his specialty.

**Kittens (inj.):** an exclamation used in place of profanity.
  In a sentence:
  "Holy *kittens*, that was godlike pudding."

**Onomatopoeia (n.):** boom, baa baa, squeal, bam, biff, bang, buzz, pow, rustle, zap, snorf, keerang, schlarggle, screech, ka-ching, dum-de-dum-dum, kablooie, clump, cling, clang, bang, whiz, swish. Fancy Greek term for *swoosh*.
  In a sentence:
  "All this snapping and slurping is making me hunger for a bowl of *onomatopoeia*."

**Groovy (adj.):** anything or anyone. Any scooch that rings your chimes, floats your lifeboat, rubs your kitten, or bangs your shiny bronze gong. *Groovy* is associated with kitschy '60s clichés like bell-bottoms and headbands, but *groovy* was before and will always be. A groove is a good thing to be in. When you don't have the groove, well, it *is* hard to move.
  In a sentence:
  "Loves that ambient jam. It is so *groovy*."
  "It would be so *groovy* if you filled that bong again with the Kush Berry Krunch."

**Manbag (n.):** the pouch where the jewels are kept. Pejorative as well. Be tender with its usage.
  In a sentence:
  "Why does this movie osculate *manbag*?"
  "Who brought the *manbag* beer? Was it that gimme cap over by the kiddie pool?"

**Manbranch (n.):** the disco stick, the candy twig, the Tootsie Pop, the appendage men focus on to the exclusion of all other things, where the action is, the blissmass tree, copilot, kickstand, love mop, little bro, the obelisk.

In a sentence:

"Thou villain, I invite you to take a beefy, nourishing bite of my *manbranch*."

**Orwellian (adj.):** anything that is in opposition to a free society, in reference to George Orwell, author of *1984*. Overused by those who have not read Orwell. *1984* is what people like to call a dystopian novel. The fallacy there is that dystopias are imaginary places where people live in fear. Orwell is dead. But rest assured, he is spinning like a bobbin in his grave.

In a sentence:

"The president used *Orwellian* logic in his speech regarding America being a defender of human rights and freedom."

**Love (n.):** We all knows it when we feels it. Most humans are striving for a semblance of it. In our current era, love is on the ropes, what with sexting, pornography, boy singers, and furries. So confusing and so many subtle variants. It is cool to love roller coasters but hard to love vultures. One may love fudge but hate brownie eaters. Love can hurt and be in vain. But it is still the most sought-after feeling. Love is why we are here on Earth. The problem is that hate is easier for lots of individuals than love. It feels more comfortable, and huge groups can do it better, plus you get to carry poorly spelled signs and wear hoods and whatnot. *Loves* is the *Smartest Book*'s favorite usage.

In a sentence:

"Oh my kittens, that leather jacket, *loves*."

"I *loves* you."

"I knows."

**Egregious (adj.):** Why say *bad*, when you can say *egregious*? *Egregious* makes something bad so terrible, it is awful fun again. Why go one syllable when you can go Greek and hot the place up?

In a sentence:

"Wearing a propeller beanie to anything but a clown's funeral is in *egregious* taste."

**Iconoclast (n.):** one who attacks cherished beliefs. This is a difficult trick in a world that requires money to live. There has been a show on TV called *Iconoclasts*. It pits two people of renown together so they can talk about how being on TV is ripping out the underpinnings of a fascist world. One pairing was Samuel Jackson, the furiously cool actor, and Bill Russell, the first black coach in the NBA and an outspoken advocate for civil rights. That seems to fit the definition. Bit baffling some of the other pairings, such as Mike Myers, a Canadian, and Deepak Chopra, the New Age believer of pseudomedicine. But the cake taker for most bizarre *Iconoclasts* has to go to Judd Apatow, a movie producer, and Lena Dunham, a rich person with a TV show. Those pairings are not iconoclasts, unless the definition is expanded to anyone who rose through the corporate system by sales work and meetings. However, since there is not yet a program called *Bourgeois Conformists*, we will have to take the Sundance Network's word for it.

In a sentence:

"Wow, the dominant paradigm needs mad realignment, maybe we should call for an *iconoclast*."

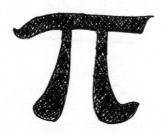

## SEVERAL WORDS *THE SMARTEST BOOK*
## WOULD BANISH

Yes, acronyms like FOMO and LOL are an annoyance for the moment, but if you put your phone down, you can avoid them. *Fail, swagger, tiger mom, cray cray, totes,* and *hashtag* are also a bummer, but one feels as time moves on, these words will seem as obsolete as *whippersnapper* and *Nantucket sleigh ride.* It is morally reprehensible to use words that are simply lazy and childish. All of the below should be avoided at all costs (though some are permissible with caveats). You have been forewarned, philistine.

**Bitch (v.):** As a noun, completely outdated. "Hey, man-bitch, nice tan." Use never. As a verb, wildly useful.

In a sentence:

"Let's have a *bitch* through *People* magazine."

**Hipster (n.):** Yes, you ride a fixed-gear bike and drink single-origin chai from a local specially abled artist's hand-thrown ceramic mug. Your bi-friend only listens to cassettes, and you just *love* vintage flats, and your rescue dog is named Cobain. Please just wear your hat and glasses and turned-up pants and defy categorizing. Remember: you will one day be driving a Volvo with toys thrown willy-nilly and Burger King wrappers on the floor, listening to Sade and digging it unironically. Even the freshest kale can go brown and wilt. *Cave futurum.*

**Epic (adj.):** 1) Appropriate if telling a story about a hero, exciting events or adventures, like Homer's immortal *Iliad*, Charlton Heston's chariot-driven *Ben-Hur*, or even the hilarious award-winning movie about hats and boats,

*Titanic.* Not applicable to your burrito or anything to do with your life. Unless you are a polar explorer or fix computer equipment in space.

2) Appropriate if describing anything very large and unusually difficult or impressive. Inappropriate for anything you accomplished or your friends did. If combined with *win* or *fail*, can be fatal to friendships and good writing.

**Stoked (adj.):** If you are a tight end in the '80s, then this is a legitimate feeling. Surely your enthusiasm might find an alternate expression, like *pumped* or *primed* or *rabid* or *ecstatic.*

**Puke (n.):** Please just be sick to your stomach.

**Poop (n.):** Grow up. If you are being potty trained, okay. After the age of three, do not use under any circumstances. Imagine if your name was Proops.

In a sentence:

"I have to go *poop.*"

"Why didn't you wear diapers, then?"

# MOVIES I
## The Classics

Come back to black and white. When the stakes were high and dolls were not always on the up-and-up. World wars were personal, like in *Casablanca*, *Lifeboat*, and *Grand Illusion*, testing people's mettle and morals and straining humanity to find its heart while enduring the worst circumstances imaginable. Honor and love and treachery and fear and hate and killing all while smoking wherever you damn well pleased. Classy she-devils like Gilda and Kathie were made to tempt the right guys. Guys who would never kill their partner over a dame—or would they? Step into the glorious past where people actually tried to be articulate and there were no Adam Sandler movies.

### CASABLANCA
**Michael Curtiz, director, 1942**

The real great American picture. Underneath the happy accident of commerce meeting patched-together screenplay meeting commercial success are dozens of true stories of personal triumph over the forces of evil. There is so much more to this movie than one viewing can contain. Nefarious drunkard Rick (Humphrey Bogart) loved Ilsa (Ingrid Bergman), Ilsa left him crying in the rain in Paris. Rick is now in Morocco, running a saloon where all the iniquitous types hang and ply their shady trades. One day Ilsa walks in, and damned if she isn't married to Victor Laszlo, the freedom fighter. Victor is virtue itself, wears a white suit, and orders a champagne cocktail. If you had just escaped from a concentration camp, would you have the sangfroid to wear white and be that cool? Everyone who worked on this movie has an amazing story of fighting persecution. Bogie was a civil rights advocate who defied the McCarthy witch hunts. Paul Henreid, who plays Victor, refused to join the Nazi Actors' Guild when he was in Vienna. Later he protested the House Un-American Activities Committee with Bogart and was blacklisted. Hitchcock picked him up, and he became a TV director. Peter Lorre had to run for his life after being a star in Germany. Marcel Dalio, the croupier, escaped from the Nazis with his wife, Madeleine LeBeau, who plays Bogie's girlfriend. Dalio lost family in concentration camps, and the Nazis used his face on posters as an example of "a typical Jew." S. Z. Sakall, or Carl the waiter, fled the Nazis, too, and lost three sisters in the death camps. Conrad Veidt, who plays the evil Nazi Major Strasser, also left Germany with his Jewish wife to escape incarceration and torture. Almost all the bit players escaped from Europe. But beyond the backstories of the actors, *Casablanca* is the great triumph of commercial filmmaking. It is funny, sad, stirring, emotional, and hypnotically manipulative. When was the last time you were proud of characters? Watch it and see if you don't well up. I dare *Citizen Kane* to make you cry.

## LIFEBOAT
### Alfred Hitchcock, director, 1944

My father warned me about men and booze,
but he never mentioned a word about women and cocaine.
—Tallulah Bankhead

Tallulah Bankhead was a hot, top star of the stage on both sides of the puddle. Girls waited outside her dressing room, and they usually got what they wanted. She was an outrageous character who makes Angelina Jolie look like a nun. Her screen career is spotty, ending with the obligatory horror movie in the '60s, but Hitchcock knew her magic was right for this picture. She is what we would now call fierce, but *fierce* is a poor adjective to describe her fabulousness. She eats men and women for lunch and then gets high over their prone bodies. She had to climb a ladder into a giant tank of water they were shooting in. She did not wear unmentionables, and every day the boys of the crew cheered her. This is her movie, and she wins it, but Alfred Hitchcock could make a movie about a sofa entertaining. He takes the one setting of a group of distressed survivors in a boat and spins it out so you are dazzled by the staunch acting and massive character development. This movie, like his later movie *Rope*, proves you can do it all in one place if you have the nerve and a great plot.

In another director's hands, this could have been a typical-for-the-time-period propaganda war movie. But instead, Hitchcock takes a story by John Steinbeck and a top-notch cast turns out a terrific thriller where there are no good guys or bad guys—just people trying to survive in an impossible situation. The set, place, time, and plot all boil down to a group of survivors in a lifeboat after a German submarine attack in WWII. A glamorous reporter (the fabulous sexpot and outrageous party doll Tallulah Bankhead in her greatest role) sporting a mink coat in the ocean, with matched luggage, has to make way for all the other victims, one by one, in her lifeboat. The rich guy, the blue-collar guy, the dutiful nurse lady, the dedicated black sailor, and finally, a German refugee—*oder ist er*? Over the course of an hour and a half, a movie shot in a huge tank in Culver City explores the meaning of life, love, race, loyalty, and what constitutes murder during a war. Everyone got hurt in the giant water tank. Broken ribs and whatnot. Wasn't it Hitchcock who said actors are cattle? In this case, they were seals.

## THE GRAND ILLUSION
### Jean Renoir, director, 1937

What is right and what is wrong when the very morality of the world has been shaken by Satan? WWI was called the war to end all wars. Sadly, it wasn't, but it was the end of empires as we knew them. Royalty, class, and snobbery have been replaced by déclassé megacorporations and news graphics giving catchy names to our conflicts. England, France, and Germany would never be the same, and the technological world of cars and phones replaced carriages and top hats. This profound musing is perfectly put together by Jean Renoir. *Oui*, his father was Pierre-Auguste Renoir, the famous painter, so they are a divine artistic daily double. What do you do when your father is a genius of painting? Out-genius him at filmmaking. This picture stars Marcel Dalio from *Casablanca* and the immortal French tough guy, Jean Gabin, sort of a French Spencer Tracy meets Robert Mitchum, or Harrison Ford meets Mickey Rourke, if you will, thrown together in a German prison camp in WWI. Aristocrats and common types deal with the ever-changing world while trying to survive and escape. Erich von Stroheim, the maniacal director of silent classics *Greed* and *Queen Kelly*, is the very movie cliché of the German officer wearing jodhpurs, sporting a swagger stick and a monocle, but he plays the commandant suffering a leather neck brace as the ultimate gentleman officer flipping over the cliché and our expectations. He dines and hobnobs with the enemy officers because they have so much in common, but does he have the heart to let them escape as honor provides? *Grand Illusion* is the end of the world of aristocrats and the beginning of mass warfare without swords and gallantry. In a prison camp we find beauty and longing. Human, cruel, lovely, moving, and perceptive about the way we are, this picture gets better all the time.

## OUT OF THE PAST
### Jacques Tourneur, director, 1947

Film noir has elements and guidelines: detectives wear trench coats and smoke out of the side of their mouths. Dirty rats get theirs, and smokin' sloe-eyed dames are not to be trusted. Cabbies know the score and will wait for you all night and hotly pursue any car, no explanation required. Kingpins send their torpedoes to shake a guy down who's only trying to make an honest buck. Not all dames are the same, some are worse. Your partner is your partner—even if he's a rat. Striped shades cast a shadow across the room. A single desk lamp is sufficient lighting. Sometimes doing the right thing gets you a long walk on a short pier. *The Smartest Book* loves film noir because no matter what you are doing while watching, someone on screen is making you look like a saint. This Robert Mitchum picture is a real slice of cold-blooded noir. Moll Jane Greer (Kathie) has shot her gangster boyfriend Kirk Douglas (Whit) in the chest. He ain't mad at her, he's just mad she took a bunch of money and split. He wants her back in the fold, so he reaches back to an old acquaintance, Mitchum (Jeff), who is now peacefully running a filling station in a mountain town in Northern California with a handsome deaf teen, Dickie Moore, of *Our Gang* fame and—yes—the coolest deaf teen in all of filmdom. Jeff goes to find Kathie, and he does find her, again and again. Then happens the greatest exchange in movie history: a pack of lies, delivered on a beach, mid-torrid affair:

Kathie: "You believe me, don't you, Jeff?"

Jeff: "Baby, I don't care."

Fade to black. Stay to the bitter end and send thanks my way.

## GILDA
### Charles Vidor, director, 1946

*Gilda* is a movie that encourages Rita Hayworth to run wild. This wild ride is one you want to take. Hayworth had the goods: stunning, great voice and dancer, and more sass than all the other WWII love goddesses put together. She is all that and more. This movie, set in a casino in Argentina to make it extra exotic, showcases all of Hayworth's talents. First, she marries for money to a strange pansexual weirdo named Ballin (the awesomely creepy George Macready), but she is really in love with his right-hand man, Johnny (Glenn Ford). They tussle and tangle, and mad innuendo flies. A bizarre subplot with Nazis jumps in, and we are off to the races. Gilda sings her big number, "Put the Blame on Mame," in a black evening gown. She takes off one glove in the singing, but we feel as if we have been under a waterfall and seen the source of the Orinoco. Boom. Pow. The colorful character actors all chime in to let Johnny and Gilda know the world is watching their affair and they should behave. Uncle Pio, the wise washroom attendant, is the conscience of the film. He is disappointed in his symbolic niece Gilda and lets Johnny know how little he thinks of him. Veteran Movie Helper Joseph Calleia (*Touch of Evil*) seems to swoop into every scene with a word of caution. Once when Ballin catches Johnny and Gilda coming home late, he asks where they were and they say they were swimming: "Johnny taught me to swim. Didn't you, Johnny?" You will never think of swimming

the same way again. You will drown in awe. And go home singing the praise of Miss Hayworth's gowns. Glamorous, dangerous,
and kinky—everything a night watching movies should be.


## ALL ABOUT EVE
### Joseph L. Mankiewicz, director, 1950

A great movie about show business, a great movie about stalkers,
a great movie about Women—simply put: a great movie. Bette
Davis is Margo Channing, a star at the top of her game. Every
night a seemingly hopeless waif, Anne Baxter, watches her show
and waits for her at the stage door. One night Margo's best friend,
Karen (Celeste Holm), brings the hapless girl back to meet Margo.
When Eve meets Margo, we are off to the races. Margo succumbs
to Eve's attention and fanatical devotion and makes her a personal assistant. But what we don't know is how far Eve will go
to get what she wants, which is Margo's life. The blinding lights
of Broadway in the '50s, when theater ruled New York, gather at
Margo's flat for one of the great parties in movie history. Marilyn Monroe shows up as a junior bombshell squired by the ven-
omous and urbane George Sanders, as the cynical, self-obsessed
drama critic Addison DeWitt. Davis greets him with, "I distinctly
remember, Addison, crossing you off my guest list. What are you
doing here?" He ripostes, "Dear Margo, you were an unforgettable Peter Pan. You must play it again soon."

He points Monroe toward a producer and instructs her, "Now
do yourself some good." She asks, "Why do they always look like
unhappy rabbits?" "Because that is what they are. Now go and make
him a happy rabbit." That's all you need to know about showbiz.

Eve is at first loyal and helpful, but we soon start to see her evil
plan for sleeping with everyone's man and taking all the good
roles. Addison sees a kindred spirit, while Eve sees an opportunity.
We watch in astonished horror as the wittiest group of martini

drinkers ever assembled scheme and maneuver their scathingly witty ways through the tempest. It has been noted this movie works on many levels; one, that Eve and Addison are clearly gay and that Margo and her boyfriend Bill the director, and Karen and her husband the playwright Lloyd, have their world threatened by the homosexuals. In the '50s, it was impossible to say a character was openly gay. So they have to pay the moral price for their turpitude. There is also an element of Women having to know their place in the postwar world of "normality." This movie kicks those notions around and scalds you with brio. Camp and vicious, sparkling and delicious. Try this gem from Karen regarding her attitude: "The cynicism you refer to I acquired the day I discovered I was different than little boys!" Movie Helper emeritus Thelma Ritter as Margo's maid, Birdie, holds down the fort: "You can't fire me . . . I'm slave labor." And the filthiest entendre in cinema—Birdie, while zipping up Bette Davis's gown: "Et voilà." Margo: "That French ventriloquist taught you a lot, didn't he?" Birdie: "There was nothing he didn't know." Eve is prescient to our "reality"-filled era, a conniving backbiter with an endless empty pool of emotional needs to fill, using everyone else to fill it. Bette Davis murders this part. Strangely, she lost the Oscar to the wonderful Judy Holliday in *Born Yesterday*, a comedy, for goodness' sake. Required while watching: a martini, very dry. If you smoke, this movie is heaven. If you don't, get an ashtray. Bette Davis lights up more often than a Mayan priestess.

## THE BIG SLEEP
### Howard Hawks, director, 1946

Bogie and Bacall had met on the movie *To Have and Have Not*. They started up an affair when she was nineteen and Bogie was way older and married. He tried to break things off and split during the production of *The Big Sleep*, but it didn't take. So he came back and they muddled on, but he boozed so much, they had to hold up shooting on this already moody detective flick. Bacall's nymphomaniac sister is a drugged-up naughty photo star (something you don't get enough in 1940s movies). Bogart says about her, "She tried to sit in my lap while I was standing up." Dig on recluse millionaires, illegal gambling joints with hot dueling cigarette girls, fake rare booksellers, drugs, and pornography when it was not called adult entertainment: this one really brings home the bacon. Bogie is Marlowe, the hard-bitten cheap detective. Every doll Marlowe runs into is hot for him, and when he finally kisses Bacall, she purrs, "I like it, I want more." Bacall is the ritzy but troubled dame who spars with him. The plot, taken from a Raymond Chandler novel, is so wildly convoluted that no one knows who actually killed the character Owen Taylor. During filming, Hawks tried to get the answer from the screenwriters, William Faulkner and Ms. Leigh Brackett. But they couldn't even guess. They then quizzed Chandler, but he also didn't have a clue. While Chandler may have left some loose ends, the screenplay bristles with his distinct dialogue:

General Sternwood: "Do you like orchids?"

Philip Marlowe: "Not particularly."

General Sternwood: "Ugh. Nasty things. Their flesh is too much like the flesh of men, and their perfume has the rotten sweetness of corruption."

Pacey, dangerous, the grown-ups act like grown-ups: they smoke and drink and gamble and fight and try to off one another. *The Big Sleep* is simply fine craft. It will make you love the old movies. If not, it's your funeral.

# SMARTEST BOOK
# BASEBALL TEAM I
## Bombshells, Doxies,
## and Dames Baseball Club

> Sex appeal is fifty percent what you've got,
> and fifty percent what people think you've got.
> —Sophia Loren

What makes a bombshell? The boom, boom, of course. These ladies raise the stakes. They aren't bimbos; they are tsunamis. Notice amid the dazzling looks and bodacious frames the great acting, smoking intellect, and genuine heart. While men are a bowl of peanuts to be nibbled at with a drink and then forgotten, bombshells are the whole package and you can't pay the freight. Bombshells are a force of nature that make you take the bad road. They are built for majesty like the Winged Victory or the Venus de Milo. Movies used to be chockers with them. They have been replaced by the sylphy Jennifers and Kates—nice girls, but that's exactly the problem. Bombshells have feelings, feelings like you should weep gratefully to be in line to gaze upon them. But as Marlene Dietrich *gerwant*, "You better be careful, it might be too hot for you." These babes will blast their way to a pennant. Suit up and let's play pepper.

## Manager: MAE WEST (1893–1980*)
### (* Of course, the ages of bombshells are irrelevant.)

Virtue has its own reward, but no sale at the box office.
—Mae West

Mae West blazed the bombshell trail. From the primordial mass of Victorian sexuality, she stormed the bawdy Bastille. Actress, playwright, feminist, supporter of gay rights. She hit it big in a 1918 revue where she danced the shimmy. She was so hot, she was the cover girl on the sheet music. Mae wrote a play called *Sex*, which got her arrested, and she did a week in jail for corrupting the morals of youth. Since this was New York in the wild days, she must've done a good job. She signed a movie deal at forty, saved Paramount Pictures, and helped launch male bombshell Cary Grant. Always outspoken and harried by religious groups, she brought the noise and exploited our Puritan misery by being funny about sex. She even cut a few rock 'n' roll records for good measure. She can lead this group of foxes to victory and beyond.


## Catcher: SHARON STONE (1958–)

Stone is perhaps the last great bombshell. Wild in the brain, insane in the body. She eats men for breakfast, and then orders drinks, then conducts an AIDS raffle. Men are not the obstacle; she simply stomps over them in her heels. Males beg for the privilege of losing to her. Strides like a tigress on the red carpets of the world. If she never makes another movie, she has already shelled you with her bomb. You would ruin your life to wait in line to be abused by Ms. Stone. Blond, unrepentant, magnificent, she handles the pitchers and calls the shots. She can handle the squeeze play.

### First Base: DIANA RIGG (1938–)

Tall, dark, and awesome, Miss Emma Peel from *The Avengers* regularly makes the polls as the hottest TV character of all time. She was in a total of fifty-one episodes. That is making an impression. A superb stage actress with loads of awards, she was the only Bond wife in *On Her Majesty's Secret Service.* Nobody's fool, never a bimbo as Emma Peel—get it, M-Appeal, Man Appeal?—she jujitsu'd bad guys, was a scientist, a crime fighter, drove a bitchin' Lotus convertible, and wore groovy cat suits called Emmapeelers over her astounding form. A feminist icon in every way. She causes you to resign your post as head of the English department because she said she might meet you for a smoke in the rosebushes. The first bag is hers to defend. She calls this game rounders.

### Second Base: RITA HAYWORTH (1918–1987)

The '40s were full of bombshells, but you should think twice before trying it with Rita. The problem is when you see her, you can't think. Starring the dazzling Latina girl they made over by plucking her hairline and dying her mane red, *Gilda* is not a movie, it is a love letter to her heat. She can sing and dance just as good as she wants, so sit down and gaze, little man. Miss Hayworth is Dresden to their campfire. Her allure is so strong she has gravitational pull. The second sack is hers to defend. She can pivot like no one.

## Shortstop: HEDY LAMARR (1914–2000)

Hedy Lamarr was a bombshell by day and scientific wizard by night. "The Most Beautiful Woman in Films" was her nickname in Hollywood, following her earlier nickname "The Most Beautiful Woman in Europe." She was a bewitching Viennese Jewish girl who married a fascist arms dealer. How were your teenage years? Hedy scandalized pictures by cavorting nude and having an onscreen close-up orgasm in a Czech film called *Ecstasy*. She made her way to Hollywood and was ravishing all through the '40s. Along the way she teamed up with her neighbor, the avant-garde composer George Antheil, and they decided to invent and patent a frequency-hopping spread-spectrum device to keep enemies from jamming torpedoes. It is the basis for what we now call Bluetooth and loads of cell phone communications. Her exotic looks made men jelly; her brain made men jam. She starts the double play and finishes you. And then invents instant replay.

## Third Base: BRIGITTE BARDOT (1934–)

Bardot's body deserves a monument in the town square. Her body *is* a monument in the town square. BB's face, lips, and hair are devastating. Her intelligence and sense of humor on screen propel her to the top of the bombshell bay. There is no ocean large enough to deter men from trying, and she don't care. Like Everest, when you are that much of a physical presence, you just are. The goddesses cry in anguished plaintive tones, the gods plan to transform themselves into mortals and try to fool her. She stays inviolate in the center of the universe. Glowing golden eternally. Don't even think of bunting on her. The hot corner is melted and stuck to the grass.

## Left Field: CLAUDIA CARDINALE (1938–)

Cute as a nymph, Claudia Cardinale has a résumé full of art films with Fellini and Visconti. She hated Hollywood and is a feminist and gay rights advocate. Speaks several languages. La Cardinale lies on a tiger rug in *The Pink Panther*. A sight you will never forget. She is brutally manhandled by Henry Fonda and digs it in *Once Upon a Time in the West*, then turns around and fronts a group of would-be rapists. Italy claims her, but we all need her bad. She has it all. Claudia makes the blind sighted. She will be an able keeper of the field.

## Center Field: URSULA ANDRESS (1936–)

There have been seven thousand Bond films and twice as many Bond Girls. Lots of foxes, a few bombshells, the remarkably named Pussy Galore in *Goldfinger*, played by Honor Blackman, who leads an all-girl flying circus, but Ursula Andress did everything before the theme song even got written. Her empire was built as the first BG in *Dr. No*. Wearing a white bikini and a giant knife, she strode from the sea like an armed and dangerous Venus and blew our minds. Blond, deadly, totally glamorous. She could make the pope rob a convenience store to buy her a trinket. The big area in center is too small a stage for what she is dealing.

### Right Field: PAM GRIER (1949–)

She's the meanest chick in town!
—poster for *Foxy Brown*

The baddest One-Chick Hit Squad that ever hit town!
—poster for *Coffy*

Pam Grier was the Queen of Blaxploitation and the first great black Woman action lead. Grier was cool as a popsicle and vicious as an underfed wildcat. She was badassery served piping hot. She always gets violent man-style revenge on ratty boyfriends, pimps, and drug kingpins. Her sexy 'fro and hot pants make all kinds of music. A dude cries out she's "a whole lotta Woman." Pam Grier is so *magnifique* that she has been brought back many times to reprise and venerate her own groundbreaking smashtasticness. In *Jackie Brown* she is sexy as hell and still outwitting appallingly evil gangsters. You need a candle and some slow jams and an iron will. In real life she was with the tempestuous Richard Pryor, so stand well back. Bonus bombshell points for being in *Scream Blacula Scream*. Right field needs the best arm. Ms. Grier has it.

### Starting Pitcher: RAQUEL WELCH (1940–)

Mount Rushmore is not as rock solid as Raquel Welch. *One Million Years B.C.* has lizards dressed as dinosaurs, a primitive form of cave English is spoken, and in the midst of all this camp, Miss Welch stormed the troglodytes with a wildly stuffed prehistoric bikini and sexy pampooties. The '60s and '70s play Shakespeare off her balcony. Boomsnackulous enduring sex symbol, she gives symbolic sex a good name. Because there is nothing symbolic about it. You are lucky she doesn't start every game with that heat.

### Starting Pitcher: SOPHIA LOREN (1934–)

Mother, actress, Oscar winner, neofascist, Sophia Loren is a glistening megastar of loads of pictures. Married to icky hobbity producer Carlo Ponti, but available to Cary Grant. Her waist is waspy, her top voluminous, her hips definitive. You would sell your mother into servitude if she batted her eyelashes at you. Mother would understand. Mad curveball. Extreme right-hander.

### Starting Pitcher: ELIZABETH TAYLOR (1932–2011)

Forget the Percodan decades, Liz has magic violet eyes and all the cookies in the shop. In *A Place in the Sun* with Montgomery Clift, she is so hot she sets him straight. A child star and millionaire entrepreneur, she took all the drugs, owned all the diamonds, married all the guys, went to all the rehabs, had all the operations, and then took names. She requires buckets of jewels and a small dog. She ate junk food and wore cashmere into the pool. Toward the end, she showed up on the patio at the Abbey Bar in West Hollywood and day-drank in her wheelchair. We all live in her wake. Just try to hit her. She has too much stuff.

### Starting Pitcher: AVA GARDNER (1922–1990)

Gardner grew up barefoot in North Carolina; lucky North Carolina. Scouted from a photo as a teen, she had the verve to marry licentious elf Mickey Rooney, revive manic-depressive Frank Sinatra's career, and tangle with contentious bandleader and snide intellectual Artie Shaw. She was carried up the steps by the male bombshell bullfighter known as Numero Uno, who also dated Bardot and Rita Hayworth. In *The Killers*, Ava makes you want to sell your soul to Satan for a chance to pick up her stockings. Satan makes a sale. She needs a drink. Our own Shoeless Joe. Say it is so, Ava.

## Starting Pitcher: TAMARA DOBSON (1947–2006)

The most elegant of bombshells, Tamara Dobson follows after Lena Horne and Dorothy Dandridge for poise and class. What gives her the bombshell nod is that she was a six-foot-two fashion model who played Cleopatra Jones, a special agent to the president, who fights lesbian drug lord Shelley Winters in the ghetto. Dobson wears the hippest threads and the biggest 'fro known to humanity. She also never gets bested by a man no matter how punk-assed, sexist, or racist, and she has a superbad Corvette with automatic weapons. She is in fact *the* bad mamma jamma. Unhittable.

## Relief Pitcher: JANE RUSSELL (1921–2011)

Jane Russell was one tough cookie and, along with Marilyn Monroe, they anti-personnel-bombshelled in *Gentlemen Prefer Blondes*, the *Citizen Kane* of bombshell movies. They dance and sing and get what they want. Our Jane is the perfect match to male bombshell Robert Mitchum. She and Mitch are paired a few times with incendiary results. In *Macao*, he is riding the ferry to Macao and looks upstairs as she is changing her stockings. Jane says, "You like the view?" Mitch says, "It's not the Taj Mahal, but it'll do." It is the Taj Mahal. It's you who won't do. She shuts down everyone in the late innings.

### Utility Player: JAYNE MANSFIELD (1921–1967)

"The girl can't help it, she was born to please." Mansfield's figure anticipates the Big Bang; she was buxom, booming, and hilarious for the win. She took Marilyn to the limit. When she walks down the street at the top of *The Girl Can't Help It*, the great '50s rock 'n' roll movie, Little Richard chants the phrase. As she wiggles down the street, men's glasses crack, and if you weren't getting the picture, the milkman's milk bottle explodes. She is also most charming and lovable. You would leave your family on an ice floe and walk over the glacier just to drown near her. She comes off the bench with a vengeance.

### Designated Hitter: MARILYN MONROE (1926–1962)

The voice, the look, the delivery, the humor, the acting, the magic, the franchise. Could only be brought down by a dynasty. A huge threat to go long every time.

### Team Security: TURA SATANA (1938–2011)

Tura Luna Pascual Yamaguchi was born in Japan, interred in America during WWII. Gang-raped as a child, she hunted down each man who did it to exact her revenge. Moved to L.A. as a burlesque dancer, was photographed by the silent-film screen legend Harold Lloyd, dated Elvis and turned down his proposal, was an expert at martial arts, and kills a man by snapping him in two in the Russ Meyer danger-girl classic *Faster, Pussycat! Kill! Kill!* No scalping allowed. She will kung fu your lame ass.

## Owner: ANGELINA JOLIE (1975–)

Angelina is a real-world bombshell. Married to male bombshell Brad Pitt, whom we imagine and hope she leads around on a string. She flies herself around the globe doing good, giving massively to charity, and forcing world leaders to acknowledge the poor. That is bombshell sexy. Superfox and unfeasibly thin, she is a superhero for being a mensch in a world of shallow blambinas. Her tattoos will confuse you unless you read Cambodian. Hollywood is far too tiny a playground for her interests. She needs a world to change the village. As Gilbert and Sullivan might have said, she is the very model of a modern major bombshell. She owns the club and you.

# POETRY I
## Ovid (43 BC–c. AD 17)

Super hot. Ovid wrote of love and *Metamorphoses*, as well as the lament of famous heroines of history, written in couplets as letters to their men. He was famous and popular and somehow pissed off the emperor Augustus enough to get himself banished to a dump on the Black Sea for what he described as a "poem and a mistake." Could the prim Augustus have not dug his love poems? Or was he too close with Augustus's granddaughter Julia, whom he also had exiled and whose husband he had had waxed? We will never know for sure. Ovid wrote plays and books and is held with Virgil, another of Augustus's favorites, and Horace as the greatest of the Latin poets. He knew from longing, as he spent years in exile writing poems addressed to the wife he would never see and the emperor who would not bend. This poem is a straight-up poem of desire, with jokes. By way of explanation, a *wen* is a boil or mark. Take this one to the pasture and lie down with it and a bowl of grapes. Jove is Jupiter is Zeus, the chief god. We all want more days like this.

### In Summer's Heat

In summer's heat and mid-time of the day,
To rest my limbs upon a bed I lay,
One window shut, the other open stood,
Which gave such light as twinkles in a wood
Like twilight glimpse at setting of the sun,
Or night being past and yet not day begun.

Such light to shamefaced maidens must be shown,
Where they may sport, and seem to be unknown.
Then came Corinna in a long, loose gown,
Her white neck hid with tresses hanging down,
Resembling fair Semiramis going to bed,
Or Lais of a thousand wooers sped.
I snatched her gown, being thin the harm was small,
Yet strived she to be covered therewithal,
And, striving thus as one that would be chaste,
Betrayed herself, and yielded at the last.
Stark naked as she stood before mine eye,
Not one wen in her body could I spy.
What arms and shoulders did I touch and see?
How apt her breasts were to be pressed by me?
How smooth a belly under her waist saw I?
How large a leg, and what a lusty thigh?
To leave the rest, all liked me passing well;
I clinged her naked body, down she fell.
Judge you the rest. Being tired, she bade me kiss.
Jove send me more such afternoons as this.

# THE WAY BACK I
## Alexander the Great
### (356 BC–323 BC)

Why was Alex so Great? Well, kids, he was young and good-looking with cool hair, a fearless, brilliant tactician, and leader of men, and oh, he conquered the world. Alexander persists through the ages, and that takes more than hot locks and bisexuality. It takes charisma and madness.

His dad was King Philip II of Macedon, a one-eyed drunk, philanderer, and military genius; his mom was Olympias, an exotic princess, witch, and devotee of mystery cults.

Aristotle (yes, that Aristotle) brought to school Alexander and all the other local princelings who made up his young posse. He read, rode, and had sex with his cohorts. Which was not unusual for then or—let's be honest—any time in rich-kid history. They remained his lifelong inner circle on his mad trip of conquest.

The golden age of Greece was finished and Macedonia, the drunken, backward, now suddenly organized, forceful cousin to the north, was taking over. Philip dumped Olympias, because he could, and planned to take up with a teen bride. But it wasn't to be. King Phil was stabbed at the order of Olympias, Alexander, or both, and then the assassin was conveniently run down and killed. CIA-style. No further inquiry. Case closed. Alexander was proclaimed king on the spot by his followers. He wanted to rule the world. Not many teens in any era have this kind of ambition, but after all—he was the son of a god, and he knew best.

Astride his beloved horse Bucephalas, leading Philip's army, and floating a huge loan, Alexander set out in ships on an expedition to Turkey. He is sexy and unfulfilled. He needed fame like a drug. His favorite book was *The Iliad*, and he kept it by his bedside. He was obsessed with being the new Achilles, that brave warrior of the storied Trojan War who, when given the choice between a long life and glory, chose glory. Alexander threw a spear and claimed Asia as his own. Then he visited Troy, where he obtained Achilles's armor at the gift shop and danced naked around his tomb with his best friend and part-time lover, Hephaestion. We just don't dance naked around the tombs of lost heroes the way we used to. At least not with as much enthusiasm.

Hollywood is afraid to show how cruel and bisexual and wise he could be all at once. Which would be ironic if that type of expression was allowed in Hollywood. He is the funhouse mirror image of every tyrannical studio exec. Even more, irony comes from ancient Greece, as does male wrestling and tyranny.

Young Alexander was spoiling to fight the biggest army on legs and fought Darius's army at the riverbank at Granicus. Parmenio, his chief general, suggested caution. Alexander ignored him and shot across the river at the head of his cavalry. The strike was so fast that the Persians were taken off guard. A sword came down aimed right for Alexander when Cleitus, one of his boys, chopped the guy's arm off. They rode up into the huge force, and the Persians panicked and fled the field. Game over. To prove he wasn't a sissy, he decided to execute the Greek mercenaries in the Persian army who had fought against him. They begged for mercy and offered to join his team. Hard feta. He had them all put to the sword. Gods don't read petitions.

Alexander next met Darius at Issus in southern Turkey. Riding through the Persian flank, he personally drove Darius from the pitch. He captured Darius's wife, daughters, and booty train. Darius sent a letter offering his daughter and half the empire if Alexander would stop. Parmenio, his main general, advised, "I would take it, if I were Alexander." The Great replied, "So indeed would I, if I were Parmenio." Later, he did marry Darius's daughter, Stateira II, and her cousin just for kicks. The fun really never stopped in the ancient times. Gods know how to party. Alex eventually bested Darius on the battlefield but didn't get the satisfaction of deciding his fate as Bessus, Darius's cousin, trusted general, and ratty friend, had the emperor killed, thinking it would appease Alex. When Alexander found Darius dying, he wept with frustration.

Egypt played right into Alexander's vanity and made him pharaoh, son of the gods. He loved the adulation and the wardrobe. Taking a small party to the oracle at Siwa, Alexander set out to see who and what he really was. They were lost and dying of thirst when two crows appeared and flew in the direction they needed to head, a decided omen. When they got to the temple, the priest addressed him as a god. He went in alone and mythically asked the question he had longed to ask: "Am I the son of Zeus?" When he came out, his officers asked him what the oracle had told him, and he cagily said he had the answer he wanted. It was official—he was Zeus-Amon, the Egyptian horned deity. Part Greek god, part Egyptian god, a pragmatic combo platter for ruling a new mixed world. He was depicted on coins in that guise throughout Asia. A horned king. Gods wear many guises.

He took a patch of riverbank at the head of the Nile and had it laid out in a grid with barley meal by his architect, Dinocrates, and had a modern sewage system designed by Crates. He planned for it to be his capital, Alexandria. It prospered and became the hub of learning where Greeks, Jews, Egyptians, and people from all over the Mediterranean and known world came to the university and library, which was a laboratory with the greatest collection of books, inventions, and tchotchkes in the ancient world. It became the seat of the Greek line of pharaohs known as the Ptolemies started by Alexander's buddy and general, Ptolemy, which ended so splashily three hundred years later with that foxy political genius, Cleopatra.

Alexander and his troops were taken to see the Gordian Knot—a massive tangle of old cords tied to a wagon that could not be unwound. Legend stated that whoever could undo the knot would rule all of Asia. Alexander stepped up, and in one version of the story, pulled a peg and released the whole knot. In a more revealing version, he drew his sword and simply cut the bastard in two. Each version nods to an aspect of his duality: philosopher and student of Aristotle, or general with a big, hard weapon. He was both—and a restless conqueror, a dangerous threat to the safety of the world.

He brought Aristotle's nephew, Callisthenes, with him as spin doctor and head propagandist. The retinue had physicians, engineers, scientists, and poets, as well as allies from the Balkans, Athens, and everywhere in Greece (except the Spartans, who wouldn't join this mission). His was a curious mind contained in the perfectly formed body of a mad warrior. His favorite pastime in between battles was hunting wild animals to his own great physical danger. He thrived on danger and was convinced of his own place in the pantheon of immortals. He was what we would describe now as a maniac. Gods are sometimes scary.

While conquering, he met a hot Bactrian princess billed as the most beautiful Woman in all of Asia, Roxanne, and he married her forthwith. He was becoming a flaming Persian in dress and bearing. The Greeks he rode with found the Persians a bit prissy for their tastes. They had a custom called *proskynesis*, practiced when entering the presence of the king. It required kneeling and blowing kisses to your overlord. Alexander was wearing purple slippers, a white girdle, and a cape, and everyone had to bow. The men were doubtful. Trouble was brewing.

Drinking continued, cross words were exchanged. Alexander was insufferable, bragging that he did it all on his own as his companions argued they were there as well. Eventually, Cleitus got well loaded and said something like, "I saved your hide at Grani-cus." Alexander ripped a spear from a guard and ran him through. Alexander was then overcome with remorse, but it is a bit tricky to unkill someone.

Alexander's bedraggled army headed for India. His ambi-tion to be king of Asia was all. But the troops had had enough. They'd been at this campaign of domination for eight years. They revolted and wouldn't fight. Coenus, who commanded the far right of the infantry, the most exalted position on the battlefield, urged Alexander to stop, pull out, and head back to Macedon to rest in wealth and praise. (In Macedonia, Alexander would never have to buy a bowl of wine again.) Alexander himself went before the troops, but the old veterans broke down and would not yield. Alexander b'snitched out hard and threatened to go it alone if necessary—a proposal that was met with stony silence. Alexander became apoplectic and hid for days, but he relented. He never for-got or forgave his army for quitting on him, a fact that came back to haunt the army. Gods don't dig being told no.

On the way out of India, they battled in a place now called Multan. The troops were not enthusiastic, so they dawdled and tarried. Alexander became fiercely impatient with their stalling, so he snagged a ladder and was the first one over the top into a horde of defenders. Now, alone at the top of the wall, beautiful and battered, white plume waving on his helmet, heedless of the extraordinary danger, he fights alone, for himself, for his mother, to best his father, to show up his men, for his wild dream of dom-ination, for his vision of a Pan-Asian-Greek superworld, where he is worshiped as a deity. A magic place where he is vizier, chief philosopher, and timeless conqueror of Arabia, Carthage, and on and on. He was now by himself facing flurries of rocks and mis-siles. He took down his attackers, including the commander of the citadel. By now, his bodyguard Peucestas had made it over the wall, carrying Achilles's shield from Troy. A rock struck Alexan-der in the head, and an arrow pierced his breastplate, going deep into his chest. Blood bubbling, he fought until he was overcome. His men had been scrambling up the wall after him, terrified of him facing the hordes alone. The ladders were breaking under their weight and men were boosting each other up on their shoulders. As they came up over the wall en masse and saw him prone, all fury broke loose. They sacked the town, killing everybody. He had his victory. Gods win big.

The army was convinced he was dead, and they knew that if he died and other generals took over that they were screwed. The troops were frightened as to their future, but Alexander wouldn't allow this. Weak as a kitten, he was taken on a barge to where the troops were camped by the river. On his signal, the awning of his tent was thrown back and he thrust his arm into the air in salute, and the army cheered in wild relief. He was offered a stretcher, but he made a show of having his horse brought to him. He mounted up and rode off. Ptolemy, the future pharaoh of Egypt, actually chided him for being so reckless in a battle that meant nothing. Alexander reminded everyone that he was divine and made his mother, Olympias, into a goddess. He was as mad as ever.

The man-god had his revenge on the army for being so willfully disobedient. He took them homeward through the horrible desert of Gedrosia, where they lost tens of thousands. Once they made it back to Babylon, Alexander made his officers marry into Asian royalty; this mass wedding sealed the deal on his dream of a Greco-Asian empire. Hephaestion died suddenly. Alexander was devastated—he cut his hair and wept for days. The god-king was apparently not invulnerable. After a series of epic drinking parties, Alexander succumbed perhaps to malaria, perhaps to poisoning (no one seems to know), and went into a sort of coma. Men filed past him in his tent, and though he was too weak to talk to them, he nodded as they went by. His generals desperately pressed him to know who would take over this vast kingdom. "The strongest," he whispered. He was thirty-two. Dead. And immortal.

A giant rolling mausoleum was built and pulled by hundreds of mules. Ptolemy hijacked it and took it to Egypt. There Alexander lay in a crystal coffin for hundreds of years. (Julius Caesar visited it in his thirties and wept, as he felt he had accomplished so little.)

Alexander is a national hero to Macedonians, a puzzlement to the Greeks, and a scourge to everyone else. His tactics are the basis for much military theory. But his own frailty despite his insistence on godhood did him in. Alexandria, Egypt, stood as a learning center for centuries and still stands. His empire broke up, and his wives and kids were assassinated in the aftermath, so that did not work out well at all. He ended like his hero Achilles—quite dead, quite young, still a rock star.

# POETRY II
## Charles Baudelaire
### (1821–1867)

The bohemian's bohemian, the romantic's Romantic, Baudelaire led the life. After he was thrown out of military school, his mom, whom he adored, and his stepdad, a French army major, packed him off to India to cure him of being a free spirit, but he jumped ship and came back to Paris. When he eventually got his inheritance, he happily became a dandy and druggie. Baudelaire reinvented Romanticism with an eye to inflame and shock. He translated Poe (whom he worshiped) and wrote his own book of poetry, *The Flowers of Evil*. Some of the poems were labeled obscene and banned by the government for almost a hundred years. You will easily dig why: "When she had sucked the pith from my bones" is hot in any century. Monsieur B certainly loves mysterious cats. To him the cat is both an angel, or seraphim, and devil, or familiar. His rhyme catches the dance, the aroma, the spirituality, the feel, the fire of the little beast. Saucy mad poet waxing in the velvet recess of the dark; saucy you pouring an absinthe into a jade tumbler, easing onto a beaded cushion, and wearing reading gloves to pore over this. From the crypt to the bedroom, Baudelaire does it all. Come downstairs and see what was once forbidden. Forbidden fruit is the sweetest of all. Forbidden poetry almost *has* to be good.

## Cats

All ardent lovers and all sages prize,
As ripening years incline upon their brows
The mild and mighty cats pride of the house
That like unto them are indolent, stern and wise.

The friends of Learning and of Ecstasy,
They search for silence and the horrors of gloom;
The devil had used them for his steeds of Doom,
Could he alone have bent their pride to slavery.

When musing, they display those outlines chaste,
Of the great sphinxes stretched o'er the sandy waste,
That seem to slumber deep in a dream without end:

From out their loins a fountainous furnace flies,
And grains of sparkling gold, as fine as sand,
Bestar the mystic pupils of their eyes.

>                   —Baudelaire, Cyril Scott, trans.,
>                       *The Flowers of Evil*

# MUSIC I
# Soul and R&B

There is no greater musical achievement than soul. Unless you like polka, in which case, get up and get me a cabbage roll. Jazz swings and rock rolls, but soul is to-the-bone convincing. You can play it on the dance floor and the boudoir, and it works like medicine. From the blues comes the pain and from jazz and rhythm come all the zest. If you have to ask what soul is, you work for a giant cartel and like it.

Sometimes you might have the blues. Life is like that. We find that blues don't cure the blues, soul does. Light up and dance as Sam Cooke sings "the cokes are in the icebox."

### WHAT'S GOIN' ON
### Marvin Gaye, 1971

The cover is the epitome of cool. Marvin, standing pensive in the rain, in a groovy leather jacket, thinking about God, war, mankind, and Womankind and whatnot. He is so good-looking it is movie star time. Marvin Gaye had been a soul star for years, the fair child at Berry Gordy's Motown (he even married the boss's sister), that amazing label that dominated the charts. But he got depressed after Tammi Terrell died, and then the Supremes took over his top spot with their unstoppable hit machine. He needed a change. Obie Benson from the Four Tops saw cops beating an antiwar protestor at the People's Park riot in Berkeley, and it inspired him to react with "What's Goin' On." He took the song to Marvin

Gaye, and Marvin reworked it into his own thing. It was a hit and from there Marvin made his opus. The songs form a free-flowing soul symphony. The beat evolved from jam to jam, but the theme is one of love and togetherness. "What's Goin' On" and "Inner City Blues" lay down the law. Berry Gordy did not dig it on first hearing. He was confused by the word *ecology* in "Mercy Mercy Me," as are all people who don't believe in global warming. Being a record boss, he was not overly concerned with a movement that was trying to save the natural environment. Gordy thought everything could be solved with a tambourine and background singers.

Now Gordy claims it is the greatest album ever released on Motown, which is a big jump. If there is a soul symphony that catches the love and dread of the late '60s, it is this record. Race riots, the Vietnam War, heroin use, and the civil war between the generations were blazing all over America. Marvin Gaye had the grace and taste to take it all on and make something groovy and beautiful. This album shouldn't be on wax. It should be chiseled in marble. Painted in the sky by turquoise birds. Or maybe strung on a wreath of flowers.

## GOLD
### Ohio Players, 1976

The Ohio Players did not sit down and write songs; they got up and jammed them. Normally greatest-hits collections are not all that, but if you want it funky, this rips. Sugarfoot, the guitar player and singer, is the St. Sebastian of funk. His jacked-up teeth, two-necked axe, and beaded denim hat announce the cool. Tortured by fine ladies in skintight britches, unprepared for the heat of lovemaking, overwhelmed by the motion of the "Love Rollercoaster," his cries of "Ow," "Yow," and decisively "Say what" will prove what many had simply guessed at: the funk can and will preside. "Love Rollercoaster" features what were thought at the time to be the screams of a Woman being killed in the studio; subsequently, we have ascertained this was not true (and at the least is a faulty business model). "Sweet Sticky Thing" is a slow jam you can coalesce to, if you follow my innuendo. Take the opportunity and make your life better. And if this all doesn't sell you, many Ohio Players albums feature a naked lady on the cover artfully arranged. Say what, indeed.

## SUPERFLY
### Curtis Mayfield, 1972

Blaxploitation was a movie genre in the '70s. They were low-budget action pictures written, directed, and starring black people. This was very new to American cinema—movies about black people that had content and real situations. Black men and Women as heroes and white people as ruthless bad guys. After decades playing maids, butlers, and eye-rolling comic relief, it was a pivotal moment for movies. Suddenly, the pictures had to catch up to the changing face of America. One of the best parts of any blaxploitation picture, aside from the plaid and tan coats and maxi jackets and huge cars and wild hats, is the soundtrack. Marvin Gaye did *Trouble Man*, James Brown did *Black Caesar*, Willie Hutch, *The Mack*, Bobby Womack, *Across 110th Street*, and so on. Curtis Mayfield was an established star when he did this score. Propulsive and urban and hip and all about life in the ghetto. Our hero, Priest, is a handsome drug dealer who is complicated like Shaft but wants to pull one more score so he can live his life. His theme is "Superfly." The cops and the gangsters are out to get him, and he loves a Woman, but it is all so complex. Curtis Mayfield's soundtrack echoes all the action and hits all the emotions of the characters making this movie like a gangster operetta set in back rooms and streets with burning trash cans. *Superfly* is not the best blaxploitation movie, but this score is. Timeless. We can deal with rockets and dreams, but reality—what does it mean?

## LADY SOUL
### Aretha Franklin, 1968

She is a torrent of song, a mighty diva, activist, superstar, and maybe the greatest singer ever. She is the link between Ella and Whitney, between Esther Phillips and Chaka Khan, Odetta and Beyoncé. She did it all for herself and carries on being one big diva who earned the right through great work and sheer awesome vocal talent. It is hard to pick one Aretha Franklin album. Indeed, there cannot be a list of soul records without her. A church-trained singer with her sisters, her father was a minister and family friends with Dr. King. She had been recording since she was a teen. This record follows *I Never Loved a Man the Way I Love You*, which had the tide-turning smash hit "Respect," the soul song she purloined from Otis Redding and turned into an enduring international anthem of female empowerment. The shouted "R-E-S-P-E-C-T" bridge and "Sock it to me" were her and her sisters' ideas. *Lady Soul* has much to love with funky-stomping "Chain of Fools" and the breathtaking "(You Make Me Feel) Like a Natural Woman." She takes the most anodyne material and, like Ray Charles, reinvents it.

## ANTHOLOGY
### Sly & the Family Stone, 1981

There has never been a cooler group. Ever. Polysexual, pansexual, funk-rock, psychedelic gospel with groovy multiracial positivity all up in the place. They had Women playing and singing, black people and white people throwing down together shortly after desegregation. Sly pioneered fur boots and giant goggle shades, the Fam-

ily Stone sports capes and plumed Musketeer hats. Rose, his sister, shouts at the world under a series of electrifying wigs, and Cynthia is the first black Woman to start at trumpet in the majors working a vest and a tight Afro. They changed how everyone from Herbie Hancock to Diana Ross to the Jackson 5 made records. All of a sudden it was de rigueur to push the beat and share the vocals. Social issues and personal worth get a big going-over, and you are in rock church the whole while. The easiest-listening band that don't play easy listening. Never mind the drugs and paranoia that befell Sly, they glow and shine and pull on your heart. Of everything *The Smartest Book* insists upon, this is the one suggestion you will never regret taking. "Dance to the Music" propels you onto the floor, "Stand!" puts you in front of your destiny, "I Want to Take You Higher" forces you to make some calls to some dudes you haven't felt like calling in a while, "Thank You (Falettinme Be Mice Elf Agin)" is a call to all to shake. Every jam will have you dancing and singing along—isn't that what music is for, to cure your lame ass?

# THE
# PROOPTIONARY II
## Punctuate with Purpose

Between the conventions of email and the stupidity of texting, it has become acceptable to use punctuation in place of finding the right words to express your pitiful thoughts. This must stop. Punctuation is meant only to clarify. And fruit off with the little smiley faces. Woman up and crack open a thesaurus for your salutations and laudations. Punctuate with care and at your own risk. You. Have Been. Warned:okay?(!):)

### Exclamation Point!

The most overused and useless of all punctuation. We get the point! You really mean it! If you mean to be emphatic, put weight on the part of the sentence that you mean to be insistent about. Use *italics* or **bold** or even crack out a thesaurus or any tiny dinosaur and discover a word that makes your point with vigorous precision. Astonish us with usage, not backloading. Importance is in the context of a sentence! Multiple exclamation points are for the very young, those who write with a colored marker, the terminally inexpressive, or the habitually unheard.

The problem is that once you allow one or two in, they tend to multiply, scattering themselves everywhere, expostulating, sounding off, making believe that phrases have a significance beyond what the words themselves are struggling to say.

—Lewis Thomas

Cut out all these exclamation points.
An exclamation point is like laughing at your own joke.

—F. Scott Fitzgerald

## www as a Word

World Wide Web has three syllables; www has nine. I have never understood an abbreviation that is longer than the phrase it is meant to shorten. I know this is not punctuation. It is a supes neg p'graph on abrevs lol.

## The Oxford Comma

Also known as the serial comma. That means it lives in a white unmarked van and waylays people and then disposes of their sentences in a mound in the forest. Nitpicky types insist that it clarifies sentences, even though it—the comma, in this case—adds an enormous amount of bloody punctuation. The comma before "and" in a phrase "The koala bear eats, shoots, and leaves," as opposed to "The koala bear eats, shoots and leaves." Clear? Me neither. I hate the Oxford comma, okra, and the people who insist one must abide them both.

## The Ellipses . . .

Supposed to break up long quotations. Herb Caen, the legendary *San Francisco Chronicle* columnist, used them in every column. He named it "three-dot journalism," and for him it worked because he also called San Francisco "Baghdad by the Bay." But ellipses smack of . . . well . . . they just seem . . . like you have forgotten what it was you . . . never mind. When in the course of human events . . . rabbit train . . . I love pancakes . . . the end . . . hallelujah.

# POETRY III
## Edgar Allan Poe
### (1809–1849)

Poe lived in poverty and agitation, and he perished delirious and raving—the kind of life one thinks of when one thinks of Romanticism and poets. Born in 1809, his parents were slutty actors who died when he was a baby. John Allan, a rich merchant, took him in and gave him the "Allan" but never officially adopted him. While living with the Allan family in Virginia, Poe heard the slaves tell stories of witches and dark magic, which he eagerly absorbed. Poe had a broody nature, was an avid fan of older Women, wore a cape, and affected a dramatic air. He loved drinking and brawling, deliberately washed out of West Point, married his thirteen-year-old cousin (though he was really in love with her mother), begged money, and struggled to be a writer. He cultivated his own dark weirdness throughout his career, and he invented detective fiction. But before all that, Poe wrote poetry.

"The Raven" is his most famous work, and he received nine dollars for it. Widely critiqued, it was a hit, and he spent a good deal of his career reciting it for people who loved it. "The Raven" became his nickname. Though he was an indigent drunk, perpetually broke, a mean critic, and a bitter pill, the power of his writing is irrevocable. . . . Poe has the last laugh

from beyond the grave. He might have enjoyed that. We have him to behold in quivering awe and terror.

## The Raven

Once upon a midnight dreary, while I pondered, weak and
      weary,
Over many a quaint and curious volume of forgotten lore,
While I nodded, nearly napping, suddenly there came a tapping,
As of some one gently rapping, rapping at my chamber door.
"'Tis some visitor," I muttered, "tapping at my chamber door—
Only this, and nothing more."

Ah, distinctly I remember it was in the bleak December,
And each separate dying ember wrought its ghost upon the
      floor.
Eagerly I wished the morrow;—vainly I had sought to borrow
From my books surcease of sorrow—sorrow for the lost
      Lenore—
For the rare and radiant maiden whom the angels name Lenore—
Nameless here for evermore.

And the silken sad uncertain rustling of each purple curtain
Thrilled me—filled me with fantastic terrors never felt before;
So that now, to still the beating of my heart, I stood repeating,
"'Tis some visitor entreating entrance at my chamber door—
Some late visitor entreating entrance at my chamber door;—
This it is, and nothing more."

Presently my soul grew stronger; hesitating then no longer,
"Sir," said I, "or Madam, truly your forgiveness I implore;
But the fact is I was napping, and so gently you came rapping,
And so faintly you came tapping, tapping at my chamber door,

That I scarce was sure I heard you"—here I opened wide the
    door;—
Darkness there, and nothing more.

Deep into that darkness peering, long I stood there wondering,
    fearing,
Doubting, dreaming dreams no mortals ever dared to dream
    before;
But the silence was unbroken, and the stillness gave no token,
And the only word there spoken was the whispered word,
    "Lenore!"
This I whispered, and an echo murmured back the word,
    "Lenore!"—
Merely this, and nothing more.

Back into the chamber turning, all my soul within me burning,
Soon again I heard a tapping somewhat louder than before.
"Surely," said I, "surely that is something at my window lattice:
Let me see, then, what thereat is, and this mystery explore—
Let my heart be still a moment and this mystery explore;—
'Tis the wind and nothing more."

Open here I flung the shutter, when, with many a flirt and
    flutter,
In there stepped a stately raven of the saintly days of yore;
Not the least obeisance made he; not a minute stopped or stayed
    he;
But, with mien of lord or lady, perched above my chamber
    door—
Perched upon a bust of Pallas just above my chamber door—
Perched, and sat, and nothing more.

Then this ebony bird beguiling my sad fancy into smiling,
By the grave and stern decorum of the countenance it wore.

"Though thy crest be shorn and shaven, thou," I said, "art sure
    no craven,
Ghastly grim and ancient raven wandering from the Nightly
    shore—
Tell me what thy lordly name is on the Night's Plutonian
    shore!"
Quoth the Raven, "Nevermore."

Much I marvelled this ungainly fowl to hear discourse so
    plainly,
Though its answer little meaning—little relevancy bore;
For we cannot help agreeing that no living human being
Ever yet was blest with seeing bird above his chamber door—
Bird or beast upon the sculptured bust above his chamber door,
With such name as "Nevermore."

But the raven, sitting lonely on the placid bust, spoke only
That one word, as if his soul in that one word he did outpour.
Nothing further then he uttered—not a feather then he
    fluttered—
Till I scarcely more than muttered, "other friends have flown
    before—
On the morrow he will leave me, as my hopes have flown
    before."
Then the bird said, "Nevermore."

Startled at the stillness broken by reply so aptly spoken,
"Doubtless," said I, "what it utters is its only stock and store,
Caught from some unhappy master whom unmerciful Disaster
Followed fast and followed faster till his songs one burden
    bore—
Till the dirges of his Hope that melancholy burden bore
Of 'Never—nevermore.'"

But the Raven still beguiling all my fancy into smiling,
Straight I wheeled a cushioned seat in front of bird, and bust and
    door;
Then upon the velvet sinking, I betook myself to linking
Fancy unto fancy, thinking what this ominous bird of yore—
What this grim, ungainly, ghastly, gaunt and ominous bird of
    yore
Meant in croaking "Nevermore."

This I sat engaged in guessing, but no syllable expressing
To the fowl whose fiery eyes now burned into my bosom's core;
This and more I sat divining, with my head at ease reclining
On the cushion's velvet lining that the lamplight gloated o'er,
But whose velvet violet lining with the lamplight gloating o'er,
She shall press, ah, nevermore!

Then methought the air grew denser, perfumed from an unseen
    censer
Swung by Seraphim whose footfalls tinkled on the tufted floor.
"Wretch," I cried, "thy God hath lent thee—by these angels he
    hath sent thee
Respite—respite and nepenthe, from thy memories of Lenore!
Quaff, oh quaff this kind nepenthe and forget this lost Lenore!"
Quoth the Raven, "Nevermore."

"Prophet!" said I, "thing of evil!—prophet still, if bird or
    devil!—
Whether Tempter sent, or whether tempest tossed thee here
    ashore,
Desolate yet all undaunted, on this desert land enchanted—
On this home by horror haunted—tell me truly, I implore—
Is there—*is* there balm in Gilead?—tell me—tell me, I implore!'
Quoth the Raven, "Nevermore."

"Prophet!" said I, "thing of evil—prophet still, if bird or devil!
By that Heaven that bends above us—by that God we both
      adore—
Tell this soul with sorrow laden if, within the distant Aidenn,
It shall clasp a sainted maiden whom the angels name Lenore—
Clasp a rare and radiant maiden whom the angels name Lenore."
Quoth the Raven, "Nevermore."

"Be that word our sign in parting, bird or fiend," I shrieked,
      upstarting—
"Get thee back into the tempest and the Night's Plutonian shore!
Leave no black plume as a token of that lie thy soul hath spoken!
Leave my loneliness unbroken!—quit the bust above my door!
Take thy beak from out my heart, and take thy form from off
      my door!"
Quoth the Raven, "Nevermore."

And the Raven, never flitting, still is sitting, still is sitting
On the pallid bust of Pallas just above my chamber door;
And his eyes have all the seeming of a demon's that is dreaming,
And the lamplight o'er him streaming throws his shadow on the
      floor;
And my soul from out that shadow that lies floating on the floor
Shall be lifted—nevermore!

# BASEBALL I

The trouble is not that players have sex the night before a game.
It's that they stay out all night looking for it.
—Casey Stengel

I believe in rules. Sure I do.
If there weren't any rules, how could you break them?
—Leo Durocher

One percent of ballplayers are leaders of men.
The other ninety-nine percent are followers of women.
—John J. McGraw

This is the toughest part of any comedian's job. Making baseball likable and interesting to people who aren't middle-aged white guys. You mean to say young freckle-faced kids aren't carrying a floppy glove in their back pocket and a slingshot in the other, chewing a wad of bubble gum and riding bikes with a playing card clothespinned to the spokes down to the playground, with a dog with a black spot on one eye chasing after to play a ragtag game of fly-up? Well, golly, it does happen. Baseball, while certainly a favorite sport around here on *Smartest Book* acres, is not for everybody. Everybody doesn't grow up playing catch anymore. Everybody isn't American, Mexican, Canadian, Caribbean, Venezuelan, Japanese, or Korean. Unlike in my day—after the invention of TV but before the death

of creativity and the arrival of the horrid app—kids today, when they can bother to put down their phones, want to play team sports where the action never stops, like soccer, basketball, and volleyball. Baseball is middle-aged get-the-fuck-off-my-lawn stuff. So no one wants to play the one-on-one, slow-pokey, waiting-your-turn-to-fail tedium. The kind baseball embodies. The feeling of standing in right field and losing your focus, then suddenly the ball is screaming toward you, and everybody is shouting and you almost get hit with the ball and your heart is racing . . . that kind of failure. Baseball is usually about failure with breaks for triumph. So it is not like life. More contained with a recordable ending. There are defined winners and losers and eventually it ends. So does this introduction. I guess what it comes down to is that I like baseball because it was something, one thing I could share with my dad. For reals. We bonded over it and I still like it. So maybe I can get you to like it, too. Let's spend a minute in what I like to call:

## The Field of Proop Dreams

It is 1967 and Young Greg is at the game with his dad, Big Steve. After driving up from the stifling suburb of San Carlos, they can smell the vicarious ghetto excitement and unfamiliar poverty of the neighborhood where Candlestick Park lies, near Hunter's Point and the shipyards. Giant cranes working in the near distance just over the right-field parking lot. A blind man plays accordion on the hill in front of the park. They buy Cokes and peanuts and see the gods Willie Mays and Willie McCovey joking in the gray San Francisco afternoon. The grass is verdant and flat as a putting green. The Giants' uniform is white with black stockings and the orange insignia on the cap. The ball is a white aspirin whizzing through the air. The public address announcer Jeff Carter gives the lineups and then sings the anthem in a jaunty baritone. Young Greg is captivated by how fast and brisk and snappy the fielding practice is. How cool the players act while taking turns swinging and slapping each other in the batting cage. No high fives. That was invented by a gay Dodger named Glenn Burke. In those days people gave each other five and ten skin, dig? The first drunk of the season is carried up the stairs. Kids crowd down to the crappy cyclone fence in right field in front of the wooden bleachers when Willie "Stretch" McCovey bats 'cause he is a lefty and often crashes one over there. Willie Mays throws a ball into the stands between every inning, and the youngsters go wild. Dirt and peanut shells blow into the waxed cups of Coke. The hot dog vendor yells down the aisle, banging his tongs on the side of a metal tank of lukewarm hot dog water the franks are bobbing in. Steve orders two and the vendor asks the only question they seem to know: "With or without?" Always with. The vendor takes his leathery hand and grabs a tongue depressor stick that lives in the crusty box of Gulden's brownish yellow mustard and whaps it on two dogs. Big Steve tips him a quarter. The buns are semi-damp, the hot dogs divine. The same crazy old Chinese man in a Giants cap and plaid sport coat three sizes too large roams the first-base seats and screams, "Goddammit get a hit" at every player. Big Steve smokes menthols and yells at hippies for not standing up for the anthem. Young Greg asks a million questions. Big Steve makes up answers. Young Greg must go back. They do, hundreds of times. Till Big Steve passed, they never got along like they did at the ballpark or like they did talking about baseball. Field of dreams, more like field of common ground and understanding. Even for those divided by the gulf of family.

The dinky suburb of San Carlos, California, had twenty thousand people in the '60s and about a zillion baseball teams. Instructional league, Little League, PONY League, Babe Ruth League; the place was baseball mad. On opening day a parade was held down the main drag, and thousands of kids in uniform would ride and march down to Burton Park with Barry Bonds, the famous and controversial Future Star, amongst them. The town was white as could be. The Bondses were the black neighborhood. Barry's dad, Bobby, was a star with the Giants and our hero. Call it sentiment, environment, the thrill of the grass, Pavlovian conditioning, call it whatever the hell you want. Baseball was all around, and we absorbed it.

Growing up, every ballplayer chewed and everybody wore a crew cut and it was awesome. Let's have more chaw and fewer incessant, revolving video ads behind the batter during the game.

## Baseball Gets Born

Baseball was devised by clerks and bank types who had played cricket and town ball and one o'cat, whatever the devil that is, and rounders, the English kiddie game. It was organized by lower-middle-class guys in New York. When their jobs let out in the early afternoon, they would go play. Then followed rules and betting and drinking and pay. Blacks were excluded around the 1880s and only Women of bad rep would attend games. The Civil War spread the game because of the idle time in prison camps North and South. The soldiers learned the game and brought it home like venereal disease.

The purported inventor of baseball, Abner Doubleday, did fire the first shot of the Civil War as a captain at Fort Sumter. He also excitingly rode with Lincoln a few years later on the train to Gettysburg to give the address. He moved to San Francisco and started up the cable cars. He also commanded an all-black unit in Texas after the war and was a raging Theosophist. An interesting person and, oddly, a spiritual seeker. He had nothing whatsoever to do with baseball. That is all made-up stuff. He was a hero, and it felt right.

The supposed father of baseball, Alexander Joy Cartwright, did play in New York with the Knickerbockers and did move to Hawaii, where he was buddies with King Kamehameha III, but he did not concoct the rules that we still use today and all that nonsense. He was just there and had all that pinned on him later. We so don't play the game our forebears did, and thank goodness. That game was slower and more violent. No gloves, no helmets, no overhand pitching.

In the 1860s, baseball joined boxing and horse racing as the only professional sports in America. The first admitted pro team was the 1869 Cincinnati Red Stockings. They wore sexy red socks under knickers, which was super hot in the 1860s. Sporting groovy mustaches and beards, the Sox traveled from coast to coast on the just-completed Transcontinental Railroad. They won sixty-five games in a row and were a sensation all over the country. Then they lost and game attendance fell off and baseball morphed into a proto league. Fickle country.

Going to a ball game was very different in the 1800s. First of all, the smells were pungent and present, sweat from the days with no AC, horse mess, open grills, cigar smoke, spilt beer from the barrels. The sounds were wild vendors hawking nuts and lemonade, marching bands, organized groups of drunken rooters belting parody songs about the players—JFK's grandfather Honey Fitzgerald was part of them. The teams rode from the hotel to the grounds in an open wagon singing their team anthem. Bystanders threw rocks and coal and every manner of junk at them. They banged on pots and pans and burned effigies of the players outside their hotel rooms at night to hector the players. The parks were not always enclosed, so long balls could roll way into the field. Carriages with gay parties parked in the outfield. People milled everywhere and were not shy about joining the action. Gamblers infested the stands, betting on every pitch. No dugouts for the players, bats lay on the ground near the crummy wooden bench and the water pail. At big games, crowds stood on the field in the outfield. They pushed back when the home team hit one and rushed in when the opposing team hit one. Players spiked each other, spit tobacco juice at the umps, and grabbed at each other's belts to stop them from running or scoring. Cops wore high hats, ladies carried parasols. From the start, vendors sold sausages, fries, ice cream, beer, and, yes, whiskey in one daring and louche league. Papers and players called fans "kranks" and later "bugs" (as in crazy). Kranks threw glass bottles at each other and the umps and the players. No one wore numbers. All the players were Irish or Dutch, meaning German American. It was loud, violent, drinky, played in the daylight, and brief; most games were under two hours.

Sensibilities were shockingly different then. Dwarves and hunchbacks were mascots. Black children were on the bench as good-luck charms; the players rubbed their heads before batting. Cross-eyed Women were bad luck, but finding a hairpin a boon. Racist nicknames were hilarious. Teams had to fight to stay at nice hotels, as they were considered like show folk or carnies. Mad, bad, and dangerous to know.

### Early Heroes of *The Smartest Book*

In the nineteenth century nicknames were descriptive and flowery. This one is a peach: Bob "Death to Flying Things" Ferguson, who scored the winning run against the Red Stockings that stopped their winning streak. Bob was an honest guy when everyone was crooked even if he had a terrible temper. He also smashed a guy's arm with a bat while umpiring.

There were several deaf players in the early game and they were all nicknamed "Dummy." Meaning the impolitic deaf and dumb. "Dummy" also of course meant stupid. Dummy Hoy played in the bigs for fourteen years after a childhood disease left him deaf. He was highly intelligent and could speak in a squeaky voice. He lived to be ninety-nine years old, and though he was born in the Civil War, he threw out the first pitch at game six of the 1961 World Series. That is continuity in an ever-changing universe. You can look it up.

Tony Mullane was a good-looking bigoted pitcher from Ireland. His nickname was gloriously "the Apollo of the Box." He was big with the ladies. He also played on the integrated 1884 Toledo team that featured Moses "Fleet" Walker and his brother Welday Wilberforce Walker. They were the first and last blacks in the majors till Jackie Robinson. Mullane didn't drink or smoke, but was enthusiastically racist and would not look at Walker's signals. He said openly that he disliked Negroes and threw whatever he wanted. He became a cop in Chicago. Enchanting character. Now he could run for Congress in North Dakota.

Pete Browning was a superb hitter for Louisville, and his bat is the first Louisville Slugger. School was an issue for Pete, and his truancy and health problems left him a functional illiterate. He had nasty mastoiditis, which made him deaf and subject to blinding headaches. He drank real hard on and off the pitch and was a notoriously sketchy fielder. Great when sober or not in pain and dastardly when he couldn't be bothered. Pete won a load of batting titles and would announce himself loudly when debarking from trains as "Pete Browning, the champion of the American Association, the Beer and Whiskey League." He spoke to his bats and gave them Bible names like Gabriel. He also retired them when he felt they had no more hits in them. You ain't seen eccentric till you met Mr. Browning. While on a night mission, he saved a child by pulling him out from under a mule-driven streetcar. He joined the outlaw Players League where he played for the beautifully named Cleveland Infants, and defected to the Pittsburgh team when Cleveland folded. That team stole a few players and became known as the Pirates. Browning also consorted with prostitutes so much that in addition to his mighty nicknames the Gladiator and the Louisville Slugger, he was known as "Pietro Redlight District Distillery Interests Browning." Fans loved him everywhere he played. He was deaf, loud, flamboyant, a great hitter, and drank like the very devil. That, my friend, is colorful. No power shakes or spinning. No Pilates and low-impact sport shoes.

No faux sobriety, worrying about drugs, performance enhancing or not. No taking the Lord on board and asking for guidance, just an old-fashioned, painful, furious, and exuberant life lived quickly, painfully, and wildly.

Was it better then? No way. No antibiotics, no counseling, no pension. On the other hand, he didn't have to hear Justin Timberlake play on the jumbo screen when he went to bat. And nothing was sponsored by a credit card.

### What They Call Dead Ball

The most awesome baseball book about the early twentieth century is *The Glory of Their Times* by humanist and fan Larry Ritter. He crossed the country with a reel-to-reel tape recorder in the early '60s interviewing ancient players in Laundromats and old folks' homes and on their porches. Players with romantic monikers like Rube Marquard and Wahoo Crawford reminisce about riding carriages to the park, watching young Babe Ruth prank on the elevator, and playing with maniacs like Ty Cobb and Rube Waddell. It is a world of checkers and blue-plate specials, of nickel haircuts and streetcars pulled by horses. One ball, black from tobacco juice that all the players chewed, was used the whole goddamn game. It became lumpy with hitting and foul with mud and dirt and spit. Hard to see and harder to slug. They only replaced balls when they absolutely had to. That and the peppiness of the pellet are the big differences between before 1920 and after, when Babe Ruth rose like a titan.

### Twentieth-Century Madness

The noughties and teens were the kooky most. Fans kicked down fences and rushed the field during the World Series. Pitchers pushed through seething crowds, and players ran for their lives after games and used bats to fight their way through the fans. "Bugs" banged on pots and burned players in effigy outside their hotel rooms all night. Today we have metal detectors and worry about terror at sporting events. In the early 1900s, it was still as wild as could be. We are and always were the terror.

Managers used wind-up toys and puppies to distract the distinctly flaky, if not fully mentally challenged, Rube Waddell while pitching. Rube was a tall, strange left-hander who could throw as hard as anybody. He was a freak even in those crazy days. The Rube ate ice cream by the quart and snorfed beer by the bucket. In the minors he would show up at game time in his street clothes and come through the grandstand taking his shirt off while the crowd went bananas. He would run and put on his uniform and yell, "Let's get 'em." He chased fire trucks because he loved to. After striking guys out, he would do backflips off the mound. The fans worshiped him. Managers hated him. He was what they then would call "touched." Today he would be diagnosed with ADD or maybe autism. He got married a lot and drank so much he was called "the Sousepaw." He passed away quite young after he caught pneumonia from helping out in a flood but was a singular star. Headstrong and unable to be homogenized.

Ty Cobb is justly known as a scrappy, violent, and racist baller who regularly slid into guys with sharpened spikes and hit black people whom he perceived as mouthy. His mother killed his domineering father when he was away at his first gig playing minor league ball. This horrible moment did nothing to help his iffy disposition. He carried a gun and fought every other teammate on the Tigers his rookie year. He jumped into the stands to beat up a heckler who had no hands and was suspended. Cobb had a sociopathic fear of failure and little regard for other people's feelings, even those of his wives and children. He drank, cheated, played golf with Henry Ford, and was one financial wizard. He played in Detroit when cars were just getting popular. He rolled with captains of industry and, being from Georgia, he was hip to a new investment called Coca-Cola. He died with millions of dollars and on the sly was supporting other players. His cruelty on and off the field was riveting to the WWI-era crowds. But he was never beloved. There wasn't much to love. 'Cause he is unsupportable as a human. But he is considered the greatest player for ages. His teammates called him "Peach," but he wasn't. Then came the Babe.

Baseball had its ass saved by Babe Ruth. The 1919 Black Sox betting scandal had bummed out the public. There had always been gamblers around the game and in the stands. Loads of players had cheated or thrown games for money for years. But when big-time gangster Arnold "the Brain" Rothstein was presented the idea by sharpies to pay a whole team to lose, the wheels went spinning off. Rothstein helped modernize organized crime because he was a genius low-life scum and evidently taught Mafia kingpin Lucky Luciano how to dress. To give you an idea how hard Rothstein was, when he was shot down, the cops asked him on his deathbed who did it: "You stick to your line of work, I'll stick to mine." The White Sox were wildly talented and grossly underpaid, and they hated the team owner Charles "the Old Roman" Comiskey. Comiskey had been a player and supposedly had invented playing off the bag at first in the prehistoric baseball times. But like all sincere capitalists, he had forgotten all about the players when he got rich.

The Sox were open to bribery; it was common and, being Chicago, the whole scandal included stolen testimony and a grand jury acquittal of the players. The wealthy white owners hired a commissioner, a showboat judge with white hair and a stern jaw named Kenesaw Mountain Landis. Judge Landis made many famous rulings and was an autocratic scourge from the bench, but his rulings were almost always overturned. The thing was, he looked the part. He was lantern-jawed and gray-haired and spoke with authority. He demanded absolute power from the owners, got it, and threw the players under the bus. Eight players banned for life, including the famous illiterate slugger "Shoeless" Joe Jackson. Ruth had copied Joe's swing for his awesome power. Jackson was a proper country boy and had played in his socks in a factory game and got the nickname there. His wife read him the papers, and he waited to order at restaurants till he heard what teammates were getting. He was the best player in the league next to Cobb and, lacking Cobb's negotiating skill, was getting hosed. He was banned by Judge Landis along with seven other guys on his team. The players took the hit for something the owners were surely on to. Notice it was the players who were impugned. The owners owned the players then and provided no health care or pensions. Injury meant career over. Still, it is called the Black Sox Scandal and not the Older, Icky, Rich, Heedless, White Guy Owners Who Consorted with Mobsters and Looked the Other Way and Threw the Players Out and Kept the Money Scandal. Oh, history, you are so fact-based.

Landis carried on being staunchly against humanity by refusing to let blacks play till he died. He was petitioned by Wendell Smith and Sam Lacy, among other black writers, to break down the color barrier. But like all great racists, he insisted there was no written rule barring them. He finally passed during WWII and, lo and behold, Jackie Robinson was signed the next year.

## The '20s That Roared

Babe Ruth started hitting the Big Apple and all those homers right after the Black Sox Scandal. He diverted everyone's attention away from the crookedness and made the sport fun. The lore of Babe Ruth looms large and has lasted way after his untimely demise. Charismatic and outrageous, he ate hot dogs by the dozen, shamelessly shagged Women, drank quarts of beer, and powdered giant homers. He stands with Muhammad Ali, Billie Jean King, and Pelé as bigger than the sport they played and more important to history than a mere athlete.

Ruth was lightly brushed by parenting above his dad's saloon in Baltimore. By six he was on the street, drinking, smoking, throwing rocks at cops, and being a truant punk. His parents were busy and clapped him in St. Mary's Industrial School where they scarcely visited him. Baby Babe George learned beautiful penmanship and how to sew at the end of a nun's ruler. The priests saw early that he was a great ballplayer, and Father Mathias took him under his wing and made him a pitcher on the institutional team.

They played all over Baltimore, and teenage Ruth, now six-foot-one and rock hard, was a high school legend. He was signed by the minor league Baltimore Orioles and made a ward of the team's owner, Jack Dunn. Ruth was, according to the players, "Dunnie's Babe." He had never been out of the confines of the priests and was as raw and rough as they come. He overate because he couldn't believe the team would feed you. He chased chicks with something close to fervency, he married a Woman and then somehow forgot about her till years later when she died in a fire and it was revealed they were still married. Of course, he was a good Catholic. He was sold to Boston in the majors and, believe it or not, was a star pitcher. He kicked mad arse in a couple of World Series and then the manager had the idea of moving this guy who always swung from the heels to the outfield. The Red Sox owner needed dosh, so they sold him to the Yankees, where he spent the next fifteen years dominating the universe. They built Yankee Stadium for him. They started winning World Series. Ruth ran riot. When he met King George V, he said, "Hiya, King." He was the center of attention everywhere he went, and he loved being just that. Ruth would yell at parties, "Any girl who doesn't wanna fuck can leave right now."

The Roaring '20s were his resort. Fancy open-air cars and camel hair topcoats. Constant arguments with the tiny manager

Miller Huggins, including hanging him by his heels off the back of a moving train. By thirty he was fat, and the writers thought he was through. But he gave a weepy speech at the sportswriters' dinner and said he would not let the dirty-faced kids down. He hired a personal trainer and went on a tear and hit all his famous homers, including the called shot, which was the longest boom, hit in Wrigley Field in Chicago. He fought with umpires and raged at fans like King Kong standing on the dugout waving his fist and screaming, "You're all yellow!" He guzzled soda, puffed cigars, and swilled beer in the morning. Children worshiped Ruth, they knew nothing of his epic whoring and drinking. He truly loved kids and really did hit a home run that he promised a dying boy. This may surprise you, but in those insensitive times, because of his dark complexion and thick lips, people often thought he was black. The opposing players let him know this through a series of horrid racist taunts. He was like Paul Bunyan if you knew who Paul Bunyan was, and he really did live up to the hype. He waved his cap when he ran around the bases, and late in his career he convinced the Yanks to let him pitch a game, which he did and won, going the whole enchilada. Ruth made movies, did every photo op, embodied the party era, and was the perfect counterpoint to the tedium of President Coolidge.

## The Depression

The fun stopped when the stock market crashed. Attendance dropped, and that forced the owners to do things like play games at night when people could go, an idea they borrowed from the Negro Leagues. The All-Star Game started in 1933, and, yes, Babe Ruth hit the first homer.

Dizzy Dean was from either Arkansas or Mississippi, depending on whom he was talking to. He was country as corn and had a wild personality. He followed Ruth during the Depression as the funnest player. His brother Daffy, who was decidedly not, also pitched on the Cardinals with him. He promised before the 1934 World Series, "Me 'n Paul will win 'em all." When they did, he said, "It ain't braggin' if you can do it." Dizzy barnstormed many seasons in those divided times with the most famous black player, Satchel Paige.

Dean was a superb pitcher and later a great announcer who made baseball popular on the old-fashioned steam-powered TV. He once said while working for CBS network, "There is a much better game, Dodgers and Giants, over on NBC." You will never find that honesty in today's game, where every pitch is sponsored and every announcer wrapped in corporate comfort gauze so as not to upset the apple cart.

Joe DiMaggio is a sexy part of American history. Tall and regal, husband to Marilyn Monroe, darling of New York when, goddammit, it was *New York*. Winner of nine World Series, three-time MVP, All-Star in every season he played. Mr. Coffee to a later TV generation. He started right after Babe Ruth split and played till Willie Mays and Mickey Mantle took over. He never threw a tantrum or argued or spit on an umpire or took drugs. He kept to himself, and the writers gave him room. He personified the dignity and aloofness of that era. He smoked and drank half cups of coffee and scared pitchers to death. In 1941, he hit in fifty-six games in a row. No one has done it since. In the minors he had hit in sixty-one games in a row. Joe had focus, poise, and grace. He is a great ballplayer, if not very modern, with his detachment and emotional unavailability. But in that, a pride that left people impressed if not in full swooning awe.

Ted Williams was known by many names. He gave himself the Kid, but writers dubbed him Thumper, the Splendid Splinter, and most best of all, Teddy Fucking Ballgame. He hit a lot and he hit homers. He also flew planes for the Marines. He was handsome and looked cool in vintage sports clothes. He didn't wear a tie. He was a sexy fighter pilot. He missed parts of five seasons serving in two wars. He was shot down but would not eject for fear of shearing off his knees, so he crash-landed a flaming jet and leapt out cursing and threw his helmet to the ground. He is the last player to have hit .400, a sacred number because, as of this date, no one has done it since. He is the consummate dedicated professional hitter. Ted possessed a frightening recall of all pitchers and a scientific approach to hitting. He was not good at marriage, fatherhood, or relations with the media. The Boston fans loved him, but the country was undecided until years after he retired, when he became beloved. Ted was outspoken and, though having only a sporadic education, highly intelligent. Ted Williams did not get along with the press and, after the first year, the fans. He refused to doff his cap in the time-honored tradition. In his final game some twenty years after his start in Boston, he hit a home run in his last at bat. The crowd cheered for ages. Ted did not appear. The manager sent him out to left field, where he was relieved by a sub, and he trotted off. The fans went crazy. Ted still did not tip his cap. Of this incident John Updike wrote, "Gods do not answer letters."

## The War and What Happened After

WWII did not stop baseball, but it was a reality check on what was happening in the good ole USA while the soldiers were away "fighting for freedom." Women suddenly had jobs and did them well till men came back and put the hammer down. Whites-only in baseball as usual, including older players and one fifteen-year-old. And if you can handle it, a one-armed man. Feel the inescapable indignity of being a star black player and seeing that white owners would rather play a one-armed athlete than have a black on the team. The owners' excuse was always that the fans weren't ready for integration. The truth was that they were governed by fear, prejudice, and greed.

The man who broke the unspoken color barrier was an officer, lettered athlete, college football star, and brother of an Olympic silver medalist. There is so much to admire about Jackie Robinson. Smart, good-looking, poised, articulate, all-around great sports star. The courage and strength of character he showed are inspiring. It had not escaped the public's notice that black people had fought in every war in the history of the land of the free and had just returned from the war against fascism and "racial superiority." Yet these same soldiers were hypocritically not allowed equal access to anything back at home. Black papers were all over this, as were the Communists, who once had a voice in politics in America. The time was long past to right this. Baseball as the paragon of all things great like apple pie, and exclusion was the last to fall upon its doops. Branch Rickey, the GM of the Brooklyn Dodgers, signed him in 1945. No one in the game wanted him to. To a man, the owners in the National League voted against integration. The common wisdom was that black players did not have what it took to play in fast company and fans would freak out and riot. The commissioner pretended to support it. Rickey had scouts all over trying to find him a black player he could sell to the public, and Jackie was quickly on his short list. Jackie was a popular running back at UCLA playing on an integrated team, then a second lieutenant in the army. Robinson had fought his way into Officer Candidate School. He had the famous heavyweight champ Joe Louis pull some strings when they weren't letting blacks in. One night in camp he got on a bus, and the white driver told him to go to the back. He refused and was court-martialed. Robinson won the case eleven years before lifelong activist and goddess Rosa Parks's boycott in Montgomery.

Rickey called him into the office in Brooklyn. Jackie had played a while in the Negro Leagues with, you guessed it, Satchel Paige, but he never liked it much. They were old-fashioned in his eyes, and he was from the West Coast and had not seen that much whites-only nonsense. He was too upfront to use the Negro-only restrooms and handle the treatment that those players were dealt.

Rickey asked him if he had the courage not to fight back for the first couple of seasons. Robinson agreed. He played in Montreal on the Dodgers farm team. They won the Little World Series, and he was carried around the field by jubilant white fans. The next year he played in Brooklyn. The other players were not all warm. Opposing players rode him. The fans shouted horrible stuff. Ben Chapman, the Phillies manager, went out of his way to call him every hideous racial name. After a few months of abuse, the white Dodgers began to see Jackie's side and started to fight back for him. They went to the World Series, and Jackie was Rookie of the Year. So much for the common wisdom. Baseball finally let blacks in, though it took another twenty-eight years to let them manage. When minorities own teams and run them poorly, then we can say we made it equal.

---

### PATER-NATIONAL PASTIME

Pro baseball is once and ever a macho guy game, but Women are breaking through, and there are a few Women playing in the minors. But baseball changes slowly. In 1987, in a press box in Scottsdale, Arizona, a San Francisco Giants official said to me, "There will never be Japanese players in the majors." This is the kind of foresight pro baseball is so wisely guided by. It is to be fervently wished that Major League Baseball allows some Women jobs as players and umpires and proves that it still deserves to be the National Pastime—a name they gave themselves. On that special afternoon we will sing "Express Yourself" by Madonna at the Reproductive Rights Dome on the WMLB opening day with Lady Gaga dressed only in a soft pretzel and President Chelsea throwing out the first pitch to Hope Solo III behind the plate. Field that dream. If not, fade away.

## The '50s and Beyond

There have been only two geniuses in the world.
Willie Mays and Willie Shakespeare.
—Tallulah Bankhead

Willie Mays is a hero. He still makes grown men cry just to recollect his derring-do. A genius of baseball, he would lay off pitches early in the game, knowing he could crack the same pitch later. He windmilled around the base paths looking over his shoulder at the ball. His cap flew off with every ball he chased because he wore a cap too small so as to provide excitement. Doris Day and Tallulah Bankhead loved him. He swung hard and connected often. Possibly with those ladies as well. He started as a teen in the Negro Leagues and finished as one of the greatest and most joyful players the sport has ever seen. He is also a frank man raised in Alabama in the Depression by his father and his aunts. When his godson Barry Bonds broke the single-season home-run record, Willie got up on that night and said, "I told him he couldn't do it, but he did it." At the 2007 All-Star game, he gave Ken Griffey Jr. his jacket, and that millionaire superstar jumped up and down like a six-year-old. That is Willie's magic. He played like he loved it. He still loves it. That is why people love him.

Mickey Mantle, the legend, the drinker, the errant dad, the belter of homers, came from the small town of Commerce, Oklahoma. His dad, Mutt, worked in a mine. Nearly every man in his family had died before the age of forty. So Mickey drank and chased as if every day were his last. Mutt named Mickey for a ballplayer—Mickey Cochrane—and drilled him endlessly, making him hit from both sides of the plate. Mickey was the best player in his tiny town and word got out. The Yankees sort of secretly and illegally signed him as a high school student. Mickey was cute and shy and had an "aw, shucks" personality. When he arrived in the majors it was evident he was the fastest player in the game and could hit the ball harder and farther than anyone else.

He was awkward at first but grew to love New York, where he partied hard and had Women falling all over him. A horrible fluke injury in his rookie season came during the World Series against the crosstown Giants featuring rookie Willie Mays. Mays hit the ball to right center. Joe DiMaggio, who was coincidentally Mays's and Mantle's hero, was playing center and called Mantle off the ball. He pulled up and stepped on a sprinkler and tore his knee. He was never quite the same, and a million injuries and wild nights later he still turned out to be one of the greatest of all time. Straight-up immortal.

## The '60s Did Not Start Groovy

The parks were ancient and crumbling. White people had moved to the suburbs to escape being around nonwhite people. TV was paying the teams more. Clubs moved to the West Coast when the owners finally awoke from their alcoholic stupor and realized there was a whole country full of fans. Blacks and Latinos were now on every team—yes, it took that long—but were still often segregated on the road, having to stay and eat apart from the white players.

The 1960s Cardinals finally housed and fed all the players together like humans and they came up with a team that won three pennants. That and the ferocity of their star pitcher, the tall, black, and intimidating Bob Gibson. He was a sickly child, but his older brother, a playground legend, never let him complain and instilled him with maturity and an uncommon drive to win. Gibson was an all-around athlete and signed with the legendary barnstorming basketball team, the Harlem Globetrotters, where he was great at dunking but did not dig all the clowning. The Cardinals signed him and finally paid him to quit playing hoops in the off-season. He hated his first manager Solly Hemus, whom he thought racist and who offered him little encouragement. When the Cards hired the encouraging Johnny Keane, Gibson's career took off. He was notorious for never speaking to the opposing players and throwing at guys' heads. He barely spoke to his own teammates on game day and hated for the catcher to come out for a conference. He told Tim McCarver, "The only thing you know about pitching is you can't hit it." He went on to win two games in the 1964 World Series, giving up two homers in the ninth inning of the seventh and deciding game and hanging tough for the win. He then put on a big pitching show, winning three games in the 1967 World Series and winning MVP in 1968, and forced baseball to lower the pitching mound five inches since no one could hit him. Perhaps nothing more exemplifies Gibson than when facing Hall of Famer Roberto Clemente in July '67—he took a line drive off his leg, shattering his fibula, and stayed in to pitch with a broken leg before the bone snapped. That September he won those three games in the World Series. That is crazy tough.

Peter Rose is a dynamo. Infamous for his hairdo and being banned for gambling, Rose played for hundreds of years and proudly bore the derisive nickname Whitey Ford gave him when he saw him run to first on a base on balls: "Charlie Hustle." Pete would dive headfirst on a steal, then leap up, dust off, and call time at the umps. He threw football blocks, tried to beat up a shortstop way smaller than him in the playoffs, played every position except pitcher, catcher, and shortstop, chased chicks, uttered the immortal phrase, "I didn't drive two hundred miles to fuck my own wife," and crouched low and whipped his unspeakable '70s mullet back to watch the pitch pound the catcher's mitt. Watching him was unforgettable. Booing him was required. Admiring his play was justified. He broke the hit record of that other great maniac, Ty Cobb. But Pete was not a sociopath or overly violent. He just gave 110 percent. He was in several World Series with two different teams. The truth is there wasn't a team he was on that wasn't better 'cause of him. He wasn't fast, but he could run. He wasn't a great fielder, but played infield and outfield. He managed, but was then caught betting, on his own team, of course. Gambling is the biggest no-no in the game. Remember the Black Sox? Pete got busted while the overly educated poet and chain-smoking didactic A. Bartlett Giamatti was commissioner. Most commissioners are tools of the owners and have the fortitude of a small, dyspeptic kitten. They have been, to a man, desperate corporate drones. They defend the owners' rights, shit on the fans, and berate the players. Bart was, first of all, educated and pedantic. In baseball, if you read a book without pictures you are an intellectual. He was a Renaissance scholar who wrote many books. He was president of Yale and refused to divest the school holdings from apartheid South Africa. Giamatti did not actually ban Rose—he got Rose to consent to being banned. Rose is still a hero to fans for his tenacious play and never-say-die attitude. He did a reality TV show, of course, and can be found in Vegas signing stuff for money. The warrior player ran into the poet commissioner and the confusion has never ended. The irresistible force met the immovable object. The object passed this realm and the force is floating rudderless through the cosmos.

> On matters of race, on matters of decency,
> baseball should lead the way.
> —A. Bart Giamatti

Like a Pope who died after just a few weeks in office, Giamatti has almost taken on the aura of sainthood; a philosophic scholar who descended on baseball from some higher level—or at least a higher level than most of the newspaper and magazine writers who quoted his pretentious, overripe prose with awe, without bothering to figure out the content of his precious emissions.
—Marvin Miller

## The '70s Were Fun

The decade that featured Disco Demolition night, nickel beer night, the San Diego Chicken, Astroturf fields, polyester double-knit uniforms, Morgana the Kissing Bandit, and the designated hitter, the '70s were the actual '60s, since baseball moves at a glacial pace.

Dock Ellis was a black man and a pitcher of some regard. He was also outspoken, drove a Cadillac with red leather trim on the outside, and pitched a no-hitter on acid. Yes, he did. Players have always used drugs, and Dock insisted that he never played a game without using methamphetamine. One June day he thought he wasn't pitching and was at a friend's house where he took some LSD. He was then reminded that he was in fact pitching that day, so he went to the park. In the stands was a Woman who always gave the players greenies, the speed of choice; he gobbled some trying to keep it together. He says he was hallucinating, could only see the catcher's mitt in his haze, hit a few batters, walked a few more, and somehow pulled off giving up no hits while tweaking on acid. Dock said of this experience, "I was high as a Georgia pine." Lest you think he was only a drugged clown, Dock spoke out against racism, claiming in 1971 that he and Vida Blue, another cool black star, would not get to face each other in the All-Star Game because they had never had two blacks start before. In the ensuing storm they both were allowed to start, a first for the great American pastime. He also confronted racists in the crowd by approaching their kids and asking to come over for dinner. The kids were always overawed and said yes and he went over to several people's houses who had called him terrible names. That is activism on a one-to-one basis. Dock was once fined by the commissioner for wearing curlers, but more than that, after he retired he campaigned against drug use before his untimely demise. A real hero of real proportions.

Reggie Jackson, a baseball phenom, went to ASU and had the audacity to date white girls. This did not go over well. When he got to the bigs he never stopped bragging about how great he was. He led the Oakland A's to three World Series and the Yankees to two championships in a row. In his twenty-one seasons, his teams went to the post-season eleven times, and he won two World Series MVPs. He went to the Yankees and fought constantly with the hard-drinking manager Billy Martin, including a fight in the dugout on live TV. His masterpiece was in game six of the 1977 World Series, where he hit three consecutive home runs on the first pitch. He had hit one the night before as well, even though he walked after that at bat. According to baseball rules, a walk is not an at bat, so he actually hit four home runs in a row on four pitches. He got the nickname Mr. October, had a candy bar named after him, hit a load more homers, and was by far the most outrageous player of his day.

## Agents That Are Free

The most significant thing that happened in the '70s was free agency. The "reserve clause" that baseball owners had used to keep the players in servitude was finally discarded. Curt Flood, the sensitive Cardinal, had sued for his freedom and was denied. But Andy Messersmith and Dave McNally decided to play without contracts rather than submit to being owned by the team on a year-by-year basis. The owners freaked out and it went to arbitration. Arbitrator Peter Seitz ruled the players were not bound, and the owners who had been hoping for more power fired him. Marvin Miller, the players' rep, had fought the owners and won. The players got the power of free agency and have bargained for lots of stuff like pensions since. The owners have kept possession of TV rights, tax breaks, and being greedy.

### The '80s

The players took coke while the owners looked the other way. The best team of the decade, the New York Mets, managed to win one World Series championship and stumbled around with their contentious superstars Dwight Gooden and Darryl Strawberry. Players were openly buying drugs at the ballpark. Finally, there was a trial, and they sent a drug dealer to jail. Several players did time as well. No owners were harmed in this cleanup. The owners also colluded to keep the players' salaries down and were forced to make small reparations.

Mike Schmidt was a giant third baseman who hit lots of homers. He started poorly and hit under .200, which is shocking, but eventually caught fire and won three MVP awards and a championship for the Phillies, who were a doormat. The Phillies fans, by the way, distinguished themselves by booing him mercilessly during a slump. He responded by appearing on the field in a wig and sunglasses.

### The '90s

Boom arena baseball was born. The '80s saw baseball losing ground to all the other sports, so chemically induced action was needed. Pioneering slugger Jose Canseco has had the brass to say he was juicing from jump street. The rest has all been chaos and conjecture. We have made our feelings clear. Barry Bonds and Roger Clemens are the two best players of their generation. They juiced. The owners knew and did not say nothing. All the moralizing in the world doesn't make them or any of the hundreds of others worse people or players. Ruth drank, Mantle drank, all the players have always taken speed or whatever to key up for games. Just like everyone in the regular, not professional, sports world.

Let's test the owners to see if they have taken drugs or if they even have a heart.

## Baseball in the Age of HD

The fact that football is more popular today than baseball is not in the least surprising. One, the game is over quicker and the season is shorter. All this makes for a much more compact vehicle for gambling. The Super Bowl provides this one-off giant hit of gambling that's worldwide, and that's what people like. That's like the final match of the World Cup or the Kentucky Derby or the Irish Sweepstakes or any of those onetime big-hit gambling events. People love to gamble on sports. It's kind of the reason why there are professional sports. It's absolutely born out of that. What about the pride of athleticism and the dedication to a craft and the discipline in bringing your entire mind and body to the equipoise of one specific task that you perform physically better than anyone else? There is always that. Plus chewing and spitting.

The game is getting better. The players are fit and they play hard. Where once everyone was named Tommy and Willie, now there are Brandons and Justins. And Asians and South Americans. Finally we are the world. This is good and right and true. Baseball is a fun game. If there were no big leagues, it would still be fun.

While baseball is never going to succeed at speeding up, we probably haven't seen the last of the long ball. Someday soon there will be a new round of miraculously huge titans crashing the ball over the fences. And we will all pretend they aren't all juiced until we don't again. But some of the problems with baseball are not hard to fix. For starters, make every city own the team like the Green Bay Packers in football. Why is baseball sacred to capitalism? If the fans owned the game, it would be possible to afford to take your kids. Please stop with "God Bless America" and the anthem. A corporate entertainment event is not a weepy patriotic rally. Why do we sing the anthem at ball games? Tradition. The last redoubt of the staunchly narrow-minded. Slavery was a tradition, too. "God Bless America" started after 9/11. Now if you don't stand up, some son of liberty yells at you. Belief systems are not your business to enforce, Paul Revere. Save patriotism for never. Never is the best time for it. Bombs bursting in air are not a family sentiment. Flag waving is the lowest and scariest form of mass insanity. We could do without jet flyovers as well. Everyone doesn't welcome the sound of our jets buzzing them. To some, it sounds like fear and imminent destruction. If you need the screaming of jets to make you feel triumphant, you are either a suitable case for treatment or a member of the Georgia legislature.

# POETRY IV
## Ernest Lawrence Thayer
### (1863–1940)

Ernest Thayer was a smart, funny, rich kid at Harvard. He was the editor of *The Lampoon*, studied with the writer William James, and was pals with philosopher and intellectual George Santayana. He also palled around with William Randolph Hearst, the future newspaper tycoon. Thayer took a year off after graduation to tour Europe, and when he got home, Hearst was running the *Examiner*. Hearst invited him to join the staff, and he wrote humorous pieces under the name "Phin," as Phineas was his college nickname. He dashed off "Casey at the Bat" in a few minutes.

"Casey" remains the most famous poem about baseball and gave us another legendary American hero like Paul Bunyan or Pecos Bill. The key to this piece is Casey does not triumph. Baseball, like life, is often disappointing. Someone loses every game, after all. Casey is the hero as washout. For a gung-ho country like America in the 1880s, this poem was a reflection of how popular the game was, the Irishness of the players, and the humor of the swaggering slugger having to deal with failure.

Archibald Clavering Gunter, a New York writer visiting San Francisco, saw the poem in the *Examiner* and cut it out, thinking to use it in the future. When he got back to New York he saw that his friend the comedian and mad baseball krank DeWolf Hopper (they had names then) was doing a comic opera in New York at Wallack's Theater (where Macy's is now). Amazingly, they were having a special crowd-pleasing baseball night. The two top teams in the country as well as the cream of New York and all the sports journalists were there in the gaslit theater while the kranks went mad—the Chicago White Stockings, starring nineteenth-century superstar and impressive racist Cap Anson, and that year's champions, the New York Giants, who had prize catcher Buck Ewing, brilliant legal mind and future organizer of the Players League John Montgomery Ward, and ace pitcher "Smiling" Mickey Welsh, who claimed it was beer that made him so good and wrote his own short poem to prove it: "Pure elixir of malt and hops/Beats all the drugs and all the drops." Had a big party to celebrate themselves, and that is where the poem debuted.

Hopper memorized the poem in less than an hour and stopped the second act to crack it out. The crowd went bananas, and Hopper recited it for the rest of his life—around ten thousand versions, according to him. His description of the night is tremendous. "When I dropped my voice to B flat, below low C, at 'but one scornful look from Casey, and the audience was awed,' I remember seeing Buck Ewing's gallant mustachios give a single nervous twitch." Let's see how your gallant follicles fair.

### Casey at the Bat

The outlook wasn't brilliant for the Mudville nine that day;
The score stood four to two, with but one inning more to play,
And then when Cooney died at first, and Barrows did the same,
A sickly silence fell upon the patrons of the game.

A straggling few got up to go in deep despair. The rest
Clung to that hope which springs eternal in the human breast;
They thought, If only Casey could but get a whack at that—
We'd put up even money now, with Casey at the bat.

But Flynn preceded Casey, as did also Jimmy Blake,
And the former was a lulu and the latter was a cake;

So upon that stricken multitude grim melancholy sat,
For there seemed but little chance of Casey getting to the bat.

But Flynn let drive a single, to the wonderment of all,
And Blake, the much despised, tore the cover off the ball;
And when the dust had lifted, and men saw what had occurred,
There was Jimmy safe at second and Flynn a-hugging third.

Then from five thousand throats and more there rose a lusty yell;
It rumbled through the valley, it rattled in the dell;
It knocked up on the mountain and recoiled upon the flat,
For Casey, mighty Casey, was advancing to the bat.

There was ease in Casey's manner as he stepped into his place;
There was pride in Casey's bearing and a smile on Casey's face.
And when, responding to the cheers, he lightly doffed his hat,
No stranger in the crowd could doubt 'twas Casey at the bat.

Ten thousand eyes were on him as he rubbed his hands with dirt;
Five thousand tongues applauded when he wiped them on his
          shirt.
Then while the writhing pitcher ground the ball into his hip,
Defiance gleamed in Casey's eye, a sneer curled Casey's lip.

And now the leather-covered sphere came hurtling through the air,
And Casey stood a-watching it in haughty grandeur there.
Close by the sturdy batsman the ball unheeded sped—
"That ain't my style," said Casey. "Strike one!" the umpire said.

From the benches, black with people, there went up a muffled
          roar,
Like the beating of the storm-waves on a stern and distant shore.
"Kill him! Kill the umpire!" shouted someone on the stand;
And it's likely they'd a-killed him had not Casey raised his hand.

With a smile of Christian charity great Casey's visage shone;
He stilled the rising tumult; he bade the game go on;
He signaled to the pitcher, and once more the spheroid flew;
But Casey still ignored it, and the umpire said, "Strike two."

"Fraud!" cried the maddened thousands, and echo answered
          "fraud!"
But one scornful look from Casey and the audience was awed.
They saw his face grow stern and cold, they saw his muscles
          strain,
And they knew that Casey wouldn't let that ball go by again.

The sneer is gone from Casey's lip, his teeth are clenched in
          hate;
He pounds with cruel violence his bat upon the plate.
And now the pitcher holds the ball, and now he lets it go.
And now the air is shattered by the force of Casey's blow.

Oh, somewhere in this favored land the sun is shining bright;
The band is playing somewhere, and somewhere hearts are light,
And somewhere men are laughing, and little children shout;
But there is no joy in Mudville—mighty Casey has struck out.

# SMARTEST BOOK
# BASEBALL TEAM II
## The All-Baseball
## Baseball Team

**Manager: CASEY STENGEL, the Old Perfessor
(1890–1975)**

Casey played in the 1923 World Series for the Giants, flipping the Yankees bench the bird when he hit a homer. He managed some awful teams, but when he got the Yankees in the late '40s he revolutionized the game with platooning and relief pitching. He pissed off DiMaggio by not being reverent enough and thought Mickey Mantle was a wastrel. When he was fired at seventy after a rare World Series loss, he said, "I'll never make the mistake of being seventy again." He fills out the lineup card any way he wants to.

**Catcher: JOHNNY BENCH (1947–)**

Best hitter on a team of big hitters, the Big Red Machine of the 1970s. Bench also ruined catching for decades by being so goddamn good. He could catch with one hand and throw guys out from his knees. Now everyone does it, but not with his gun.

### First Base: LOU GEHRIG (1903–1941)

He gave the best dying speech in baseball history, and he could larrup, as the old-time sportswriters said. His old-school German mother brought bags of eels into the Yankee clubhouse as a treat. He was so dominant no one objected.

### Second Base: LITTLE JOE MORGAN (1943–)

An annoying announcer, he was a superb all-around player. He could run, hit, steal, and win pennants all while being munchkin-sized. Every team he played for was better because he was on it. Arm flapping at the dish and stealing with ease despite his lack of speed. He was the hustlingest and bright as the Dickens.

### Third Base: MIKE SCHMIDT (1949–)

Bill James said that if Schmidt had hit .320, he would be the greatest player of all time. There have been better fielders, but none could slug and field the way Schmitty did. Sorry, George Brett and Brooks Robinson. You are both still divine.

### Shortstop: HONUS WAGNER (1874–1955)

Sorry, Jeter, you have more rings, but the Flying Dutchman was simply the best player in baseball. He played virtually every position before settling at shortstop and was beloved all over the country. When he quit playing, he was a coach and talked baseball with the fans throughout the game and after over beers. One of the kindest men who ever played.

### Right Field: BABE RUTH (1895–1948)

You need reasons? Ninety-seven wins as a pitcher, 714 home runs as a player. Everyone in the league made more money because of him. He ate every pancake, shagged every doll, drank every beer, and made time for every kid. He called the president "Prez." Drove an open-air car and wore driving gloves while smoking a cigar. Awesome.

### Center Field: WILLIE MAYS (1931–)

Center is crowded. Mantle and DiMaggio won more champion-ships. But Mays was the most infectious player to strap on cleats. Hat flying, arms windmilling, smile blazing; he did everything with daring and great skill. A genius of the game and the biggest drawing card in his era. Willie Mays is baseball.

### Left Field: HENRY AARON (1934–)

A giant of a human. Soft-spoken, sensitive, and smart as a whip, Aaron was the first to break Ruth's home-run mark, for which he endured vile death threats and came through with dignity. Superb outfielder, awesome slugger, enlightened executive, great human being.

## STARTERS

### Left Hander: SANDY KOUFAX (1935–)

Unbeatable after he learned control. Sensitive and intelligent. Quit before he was hurt for a lifetime. Four no-hitters in consecutive years. He also threw a perfect game. Huge hands that can hold five balls at once. All you can say is "Wow."

### Right Hander: WALTER JOHNSON (1887–1946)

Johnson had 417 wins for a mediocre team, the Washington Senators—"First in war, first in peace, and last in the American League." Republican. Nice guy. Deadly fastball. Threw sidearm buggy-whip style.

### Relief: MARIANO RIVERA (1969–)

He was just the living end to a game. Played till he was a hundred, almost.

### BULLPEN

### BOB GIBSON (1935–)

He also makes All-Time Controversial Team, but you want him on yours.

### TOM SEAVER (1944–)

Tom Terrific to you, mortal. Miracle Mets and just plain great.

## CY YOUNG (1867–1955)

When they name the award after you, then he sits. Until then, stand in breathless wonder.

## ROLLIE FINGERS (1946–)/DENNIS ECKERSLEY (1954–)

Two A's, two unforgettable mustaches. Lots of saves.

## BENCH

### Outfielder MICKEY MANTLE (1931–1995)

He is a titan, best hurt player ever. If not hurt, best player ever.

### Outfielder ROBERTO CLEMENTE (1934–1972)

The first, greatest Latin player. Fierce, dedicated, and proud.

### Outfielder TED WILLIAMS (1918–2002)

Fuck you if he don't.

### Outfielder BARRY BONDS (1964–)

Super fuck you.

### Infielder WILLIE McCOVEY (1938–)

It is my book.

### Infielder DEREK JETER (1974–)

He has the rings and all the shiny things. Dated the world. Saved the franchise.

### Infielder JACKIE ROBINSON (1919–1972)

Put the *Brave* in Home of the Brave.

### Catcher ROY CAMPANELLA (1921–1993)

Campy won three MVPs catching.

# MOVIES II
## Buddy Movies

### SOME LIKE IT HOT
### Billy Wilder, director, 1959

Billy Wilder wrote and directed this monument to farce. Can two guys in drag be hilarious for a whole movie? This is the test case and ultimate winner. Joe and Jerry (Tony Curtis and Jack Lemmon) are two down-and-out musicians who accidentally witness the St. Valentine's Day massacre in gangland Chicago and are forced to hide in an all-girl jazz band with Marilyn Monroe. Jack Lemmon turns out to be a bold, brassy girl, while Tony Curtis is a prissy boots. Marilyn is hilarious and vulnerable and wears some shocking gowns that defy gravity and the censors. One day when trying on their gowns, the costumer, Orry-Kelly (who also did *Casablanca* and *An American in Paris*), said to Marilyn, "Tony has a better-looking ass than you." She opened her top and said, "But he doesn't have tits like these." Wilder saw Joe E. Brown at a Dodger game and cast him as the lecherous millionaire Osgood, who hits on Jack Lemmon, and Lemmon seems to love it.

The lines come rapid-fire. "Why would a fella marry another fella?" "Security." Marilyn sings and Tony does a spot-on Cary Grant, and George Raft, the tough guy of tough guys, makes an elegant gangster. Watch closely when he kicks a toothpick out of a dead rival's mouth. That, my friends, is a dancer kick. He also taught Jack Lemmon and Joe E. Brown how to do the tango. Classic American comedy.

## BUTCH CASSIDY AND THE SUNDANCE KID
### George Roy Hill, director, 1969

The funnest buddy movie, period. A sentimental favorite of *The Smartest Book*, as we saw it as a child a gajillion times. Redford and Newman, hot in their '60s hairdos and corduroy cowboy coats, are the most offhand outlaws at the end of the Wild West. The picture starts with a silent film of our antiheroes to set up that time has passed them by. They belong to the Old West, where robbing banks and jacking trains was what bad guys did. Butch and Sundance were real bad guys from the end of the Wild West. They looted and shooted and robbed trains and hid in the hills of Wyoming and Montana. They consorted with sharps and wore derby hats to take their gang pictures. Then they split for Bolivia, robbed them of their silver, and then disappeared for good. Some people say they were killed by *federales*; others say they escaped to South America, made their way back to the States, and hid under assumed names. This movie provides an answer and, because it is the '60s, it's a freeze-frame. Thelma and Louise on horseback. Butch and Sundance love each other while keeping up a constant flow of sarcasm. Redford tells Newman, the erstwhile brains of the duo, "You just keep thinking, Butch, that's what you're good at." If only he could have thought them back in time to where they might have fit. A bicycle serves as a cinematic metaphor to let you know the times are changing. Their man love is tested by almost dying at the hands of a mysterious posse that won't stop chasing them. It becomes an existential race between their egos and guile and the posse's determined doggedness in running them down. "Who are those guys?" they wonder again and again. The facelessness of the lawmen adds to the dread and helplessness of our sexy leads as they try to live their lives while committing crime, which they admit is just so they don't have to work. William Goldman wrote a cracking screenplay full of jokes and moments and random violence to keep it real. Every small part in this movie is manned by Movie Helpers: the hilarious comedian Kenneth Mars (*Young Frankenstein, What's Up, Doc?*) as the blowhard sheriff, Henry Jones as the oily bike salesman, Jeff Corey as the grumpy lawman who foretells their untimely fate, Cloris Leachman as the giddy soiled dove Butch tries to make out with before his time is up. The stunning backdrops and our groovy leads carry the day. Can they make it home? What is home when you are on the run? Stand by for a Burt Bacharach hit song video and several musical sequences.

## THELMA & LOUISE
### Ridley Scott, director, 1991

Geena Davis and Susan Sarandon are magically and sadly cast for their only time together as two Women on the run from the aftermath of shooting a rapist. The assault is quite unnerving, but the rapist deserves it. Even the waitress at the bar says so. It's a great running look at how unfair and complex the act of defending yourself is for Women. They decide to have a holiday and leave Louise's sexist d-bag of a husband with just a note and dinner in the microwave. The great Harvey Keitel works as a beagle of a tough, sensitive Arkansas detective who knows the horrible truth about Louise's past. The one who drives her to run when someone else might stay and try to explain. Ridley Scott stretches the screen to include the whole damn road, and the characters change into different people before your eyes. A moonlit scene in the 1966 Thunderbird rag top, gazing into Susan Sarandon's wonder-filled blue eyes while Marianne Faithfull sings the poignant "The Ballad of Lucy Jordan" is close to poetry. The Women start out honest, but circumstance forces them to evolve quickly into the lawless wild chicks the feds seem to believe they are. After a robbery comes this exhilarating exchange: Louise: "Why are you driving so fast?" Thelma: "I want to put some distance between us and the scene of our last goddamn crime."

The revenge they wreak on bad husbands, pig truck drivers, sexist police, deadbeat boyfriends, and an uncaring world make this one especially rewarding. Geena Davis has a romp with a young and very fresh-out-of-jail Brad Pitt. It proves Brad is funny and better as a character actor than leading man, when he always seems so droopy. It is one of the best crime movies because our heroes are the victims *and* the perpetrators, and at no point are we not rooting for them. You will consider changing your life and taking to the road in a bitchin' convertible. Butch and Sundance in a Thunderbird. Special bonus pot-smoking rasta gag late in the movie.

## THE MAN WHO WOULD BE KING
### John Huston, director, 1975

*The Man Who Would Be King*, starring the devastatingly rugged Sean Connery and the very clever Michael Caine, plays like an old-time movie as John Huston wanted to make it in the '40s with Gable and Bogart, but only got around to it in the '70s. The film is based on the short novel by Rudyard Kipling about the true-life maniac Josiah Harlan, an American who went to Afghanistan and waged his own war, and is all the more charming for it. Chemistry is the key; Caine and Connery fight the elements, ravines, avalanches, the natives, fate, and their own greed and egos. Sean Connery is the sexiest and most charismatic of actors. His greatest ability as a performer is his unlimited capacity for adoration. Good, old-fashioned movie racism and high adventure. Don't call in; it's just for fun. This adventure buddy movie is about love, the boys' for each other, the love of glory, and our love for them even though we know good and well they are shady and nefarious scoundrels. Connery sets just the right tone as the kingish Danny, and Caine is guile itself as the canny and crafty Cockney Peachy trying to work a sticky situation into a fortune. Movie Helper Saeed Jaffrey from all the old Merchant Ivory movies is Billy Fish, the last survivor of a previous expedition, who becomes their translator and guide through the strange, superstitious, magical, cruel mountain country at the roof of the world, Kafiristan. They face the very wrath of the gods, all to bring back the treasure hidden by Alexander the Great. Butch Cassidy in the Hindu Kush. Thelma and Louise on a mule with Martini rifles. You need the high adventure. You will cry at their dreams coming all undone.


## POINT BREAK
### Kathryn Bigelow, director, 1991


Kathryn Bigelow is the only Woman director as of this writing to win an Oscar, so we may safely assume that the Academy Awards are amazingly open-minded and even-handed. She directed the intense war story *The Hurt Locker* and the acclaimed torture-licious *Zero Dark Thirty*. But her magnum opus is the '90s bromance that will never die, *Point Break*. Keanu Reeves and Patrick Swayze at their hunkiest surf, play overaggressive touch football, fight, dive from planes, drink Mexican beers, rob banks, battle a gang of evil surfers, call each other *compadre*, and generally fall in love. They aren't gay because it's a Hollywood movie, so they don't have sex. They do what straight men do when they are in need: they tumble, fight, and do extreme sports. Patrick Swayze is Bodhi (it's short for Bodhisattva), the spiritual, vaguely Buddhist leader of a gang of bank-robbing surfers called the Ex-Presidents. They wear awesome rubber masks of Carter, Reagan, LBJ, and Nixon to add to the real. Keanu is Johnny Utah—of course he is—a young hot-shot former Heisman Trophy–winning quarterback turned FBI agent (aren't they all?), who is assigned to the case and partnered with live-wire foul-up Gary Busey (Pappas). You still aren't on board? It gets gooder. Johnny infiltrates the gang by dating Bodhi's ex-girlfriend, Tyler (Lori Petty), who works at a hamburger stand at the beach where they surf. Johnny hides that he is an FBI agent from Tyler and grows ever closer to Bodhi, going night-surfing, sky diving, and chasing his gang around during a series of astounding action set pieces. Gas stations are burned and pit bulls are thrown. Bodhi tries one last heist that goes horribly wrong, and he makes Johnny join his gang for it. This is their prom. Much shooting and dead gang members later, Johnny runs Bodhi down and finds out he has kidnapped Tyler—whom we have largely forgotten about at this juncture—and Johnny must save her. Keanu jumps from a plane without a parachute to get his man, Pat Swayze. It happened. The love story here is between the morally upright Johnny and the dark rebel Bodhi. In the end they marry briefly by sharing handcuffs, and one walks on while the other seeks enlightenment. When someone has to throw a backward scissor kick in tai chi pants, Pat Swayze is your man. The best action movie for stoners ever. The best stoner movie for action fans ever. *Vaya con Dios*, brah.

## A HARD DAY'S NIGHT
### Richard Lester, director, 1964

Total, tasty teen excitement with the cutest, funniest band ever. They wear super-bitchin' boots and ties and cute hats. They run, jump, gambol, leap, goof, and invent the music video. The Beatles mock television, trends, and commercialism while being in on the joke of being the most popular thingy in the world. They're always cynical and funny, which is what distinguished them from all other bands. That, and they evolved socially and musically with every album. John is the disbelieving snarky one, Paul is the lovable mophead, George is the knowing cute one, and Ringo is the best actor. For real. If you have not seen this, it may explain the Beatles to you better than any one thing they did. They made the Cold War world laugh hysterically when the world needed it. They made rock fun again when we were getting snowed in by boy singers named Bobby. Most of all, they will make you smile. Name another band that evokes that particular reaction. The Stones make you feel cool and like hitting someone, the Velvet Underground makes you want to smoke and be hateful, the Beach Boys make you want to get them a new wardrobe, but the Beatles are shaggable and the songs are tremendous. Unbeatable. Beatleable.

# THE SMARTEST
# LITTLE BOOK OF
# BOOK REVIEWS

After the disappointment of this "book," I can offer you the small solace of some books that I can vouch are actually illuminating and you won't have to work very hard to understand why. You like reading or you wouldn't be here. But we live in a world where our attention spans last less than the length of an Internet ad. So I am here to help by boiling down some of what I think of as classics to a paltry but amazingly descriptive few lines. It is literally the least I can do. Without further ado, the squint-and-you-miss-it Little Book of Littler Book Reviews.

### Blood Meridian, or
### The Evening Redness in the West

War was always here. Before man was, war waited for him.
The ultimate trade awaiting its ultimate practitioner.
—Cormac McCarthy (1933–)

{ A violent tween joins a horrific band of
doomed scalp hunters and the fun starts there.
*Moby-Dick* in the Old West with beheadings. }

Cormac McCarthy makes himself hard to read. Women in general are not huge fans. He believes that punctuation is "tyranny," and he would never use a semicolon. Quotation marks are out of the question, so when you read him, you must do a lot of heavy attributive lifting. That and the fact that lots of it is in Spanish, which he learned to write for this book. Cormac has been poor and struggling as well as granted with genius money. It doesn't seem to change his outlook. And he makes no bones that he does not care for authors who do not deal with death. He is also reclusive in the sense that he cares not at all about doing interviews to promote his work. In our post-Kardashian world, that makes him a hermit. He did go on *Oprah*, where he looked furtive, and she actually posed the probing question of how did he get his ideas. Contentious late-in-life genius or overreaching genre-ist with a violence fixation? This is your call, baby. You must deal with lots of death in this one, so saddle up and amigo, *buena suerte*.

### The Rock of Tanios

All pleasures must be paid for,
do not despise those that state their price.
—Amin Maalouf (1949–)

{ A tragic story of mistaken identity and revenge set in colonial Lebanon full of sheikhs and beauties. A strangely uplifting work scented with pine and coffee. }

Amin Maalouf is a Christian author from Lebanon. He was a journalist who covered the fall of Saigon and interviewed Indira Gandhi. He left Lebanon for good during the 1975 civil war and moved to Paris and now writes in French. He has been wildly celebrated and definitely brings a unique, colorful, intellectual perspective to religion, race, and identity. As he puts it: "The fact of simultaneously being Christian and having as my mother tongue Arabic, the holy language of Islam, is one of the basic paradoxes that have shaped my identity." Paradox is his chocolate box.

## The Great Gatsby

In his blue gardens men and girls came and went like moths among the whisperings and the champagne and the stars.
—F. Scott Fitzgerald (1896–1940)

{ Shallow, brittle rich people drink, dance, and have unrepentant sex with the underclass in the Roaring '20s. Just desserts are served. }

F. Scott Fitzgerald was a drunk married to a crazy person. He was from a notable family but was always after money. He hobnobbed with all the heavyweights of the '20s and sold his soul to Hollywood. He made it to the semi–rock star age of forty-four. He wrote *Gatsby* in the '20s, but it was not a commercial success till the '40s, when soldiers overseas were given copies. Somewhere around 150,000 books were handed to GIs during WWII. Then it became part of high school curriculums in the '50s and voilà, the Great American Novel was reborn. Fitzgerald knew all about his subject matter, the new rich: he lived on Long Island where he soiréed; when in Europe, he and his wife, Zelda, sponged off many rich friends. He was a mordant observer of the rich while at the same time something of an admirer and sycophant. He certainly comes closer than any other novelist in capturing hedonism, which he practiced, and as well as despair, which he became an expert on. As he says in "The Rich Boy": "Let me tell you about the very rich. They are different from you and me. They possess and enjoy early, and it does something to them, makes them soft, where we are hard, and cynical where we are trustful, in a way that, unless you were born rich, it is very difficult to understand."

### Bruges-la-Morte

Bruges was his dead wife. And his dead wife was Bruges. The two were untied in a like destiny. It was Bruges-la-Morte, the dead town entombed in its stone quais, with the arteries of its canals cold once the great pulse of the sea had ceased beating in them.
—Georges Rodenbach (1855–1898)

{ Depressed neurotic weirdo seeks replacement for dead wife, then freaks out when she is an uncontrollable bummer. }

Georges Rodenbach is considered a symbolist, which is to say not a realist. Feeling, art, and aesthetics come first before authenticity. His tomb in the Père Lachaise Cemetery in Paris with his green corpse spirit flying out of the ground is the most over-the-top spookarama this side of the Haunted Mansion in Disneyland. The symbolist movement included writers (Gabriele D'Annunzio), playwrights (Nobel Prize winner Maurice Maeterlinck), painters (Gustave Moreau), poets (Arthur Rimbaud), philosophers (Arthur Schopenhauer), and composers (Claude Debussy). This is the first novel to be printed with photos; that, *mon ami,* is *très moderne.*

## 1984

If you want to keep a secret
you must also hide it from yourself.
—George Orwell (1903–1950)

{ Trouble and torture in the future for truth-
seeker Winston Smith when the past is denied
and the news is written by the government. }

Orwell lived it. He was a poor rich person who was sent to a hideous boarding school that he hated, was a police superintendent in Burma, lived among the wretched poverty and squalor of London and Paris, was shot in the throat in the Spanish Civil War, wrote literary criticism, was married while in the hospital, smoked like a chimney, and suffered and died of TB at the age of forty-six. He also wrote loads of articles, pieces, essays, columns, and diatribes, including how to make a perfect cup of tea and the immortal classic *Animal Farm*: "Some animals are more equal than others." Plus the Big Boy, *1984*. He was famous and well off when he passed but had no idea how huge *1984* would become as *the* novel of dystopia. He would have been thrilled. Maybe not so thrilled that there is an inane reality show with people under constant surveillance called *Big Brother*. Neither are we, for that matter.

## *I, Claudius*

I was thinking, "So, I'm Emperor, am I? What nonsense!
But at least I'll be able to make people read my books now."
—Robert Graves (1895–1985)

{ Stuttering Roman noble is forced to take over
the Empire after his nephew, the over-the-
top pervert emperor Caligula, is rubbed out. }

Graves was severely wounded at the Battle of the Somme in WWI. He came home shell-shocked and exhausted from the Spanish flu, the virus that wiped out somewhere in the neighborhood of two and a half percent of the world's population. He was pals at Oxford with T. E. Lawrence—yes, Lawrence of Arabia—with whom he chatted about poetry and apparently played pranks. That had to be a good time. Graves wrote a popular bio of Lawrence and then his own memoir of the war, *Goodbye to All That*. He went through a couple of wives, moved to Majorca, and used his extensive knowledge of classical literature and history to write *I, Claudius*. It was a hit, so of course he said he wrote it for money so no one could enjoy themselves. Despite his snipe for it, it is well witty.

## *Dancing Bear*

I had done either too much coke or too little,
a constant problem in my life.
—James Crumley (1939–2008)

{ Chandler with snow tires. And a giant duffel
bag full of drugs and guns in the trunk. }

Crumley was never a bestseller. He put it more starkly: "I'm not middlebrow and middle class. Sure, I'd like it if more people read the books. My children would like it. My ex-wives would like it. But that's just not what I'm about." The heir to Chandler and all that is hard-boiled, he had five wives and an enthusiasm for alcohol. He served in the army in the Philippines and wrote his only non-detective novel, *One to Count Cadence*. His detectives are hard drinking and very druggy, in reflection of his own tastes, we presume. Spent forever writing screenplays that never got made. He had to be satisfied with being a brilliant stylist.

## "The Sneetches"
### *The Sneetches and Other Stories*

Now, the Star-Belly Sneetches had bellies with stars.
The Plain-Belly Sneetches had none upon thars.
—Dr. Seuss (1904–1991)

{ Fury on the beach when race and identity are explored in this hilarious Holocaust allegory for kids. }

The greatest of all children's writers—sorry, J. K. Rowling. Theodor Geisel's middle name was Seuss, his family was from Germany, and they pronounced it *Zoice*. He was an indifferent scholar at Dartmouth, but he loved to draw. He was a struggling artist living in a walkup on the Lower West Side when he did a cartoon of a knight with a can of bug spray saying, "Darn it all, another dragon. And just after I'd sprayed the whole castle with Flit!" The wife of an ad exec saw the cartoon, and he started a cartoon ad campaign. The slogan was "Quick, Henry, the Flit!" The campaign was super popular; it was the "Got milk?" of the way back. He was an ad man for thirty years while writing various children's books. Then in 1957, *The Cat in the Hat* sold a million copies, and he was now a brand as well as an author. He felt strongly that kids should read, think for themselves, and not be patronized. Generations have grown up on his humanist poetry. Dr. Seuss wrote children's books about the power structure (*Yertle the Turtle*), nuclear war (*Horton Hears a Who* and *The Butter Battle Book*), and the environment (*The Lorax*). His wordplay and fantastical names are part of the culture now. He gave us *nerd*. Most of all, he encouraged everyone to try independent critical thought, "Think left and think right/and think low and think high/Oh, the THINKS you can think up if only you try!"

### The Master and Margarita

Manuscripts don't burn.
—Mikhail Bulgakov (1891–1940)

{ Moscow goes crazy when the devil appears with a talking cat. }

Bulgakov was first a doctor who was horribly injured in WWI and became a morphine addict. He joined the White Army but was forced to be a physician for all sides in the Communist Revolution. He then became a journalist, later moving to Moscow, and finally a dissident playwright. His plays were popular, but the Communist powers were always banning him. Except, most extraordinarily, the dictator and genocidal strongman Josef Stalin. Stalin loved his work and said of him that he was above labels like left and right. The secret police interrogated him and

confiscated his work. Desperate and broke and unable to get his plays produced, he wrote Stalin and begged, "Let me out of the Soviet Union, or restore my work at the theaters." Stalin actually phoned him, which must have been startling, and got him a job at a small theater. Bulgakov married his third wife, Yelena Shilovskaya, and she is the inspiration for Margarita in the novel. In the novel, Margarita makes a deal with the devil to be with her beloved, the Master, who is in an institution where he believes his lengthy book has been burned. In the end, we find out a truth about manuscripts. Originally written before Bulgakov's early death in 1940, the book was finally released in two parts in the '60s. Marianne Faithfull got hip to it and gave it to her boyfriend, Mick Jagger, who ran out and wrote "Sympathy for the Devil" after reading it. This may be the most popular Russian novel of all time.

### After Claude

There are times when I'd rather converse
with a crazed mugger than reason with myself.
—Iris Owens (1929–2008)

{ Starts with the line, "I left Claude, the French rat." Then we are off to the madhouse. Snarking jacket required. }

Iris Owens went to Barnard and then moved to Paris, where she took up with Scottish Beat writer Alexander Trocchi. She wrote kinky art porn under the name Harriet Daimler. She had loads of admirers, such as Beckett, as she was witty and sexy, but outside of erotica, she simply could not be bothered to write. Prodded

to pen this frenzied short novel, she hated her publisher and only wrote one other book. She said about herself, "I was very involved in being an elegant failure."

## *Heart of Darkness*

There is a taint of death, a flavor of mortality in lies— which is exactly what I hate and detest in the world— what I want to forget.
—Joseph Conrad (1857–1924)

{ Mayhem in colonial Africa ensues when a corporate underling is sent up a steamy jungle river to stop a crazed boss. }

Joseph Conrad was born into a Polish family when Russia was dominating Poland. His dissident parents were forced into exile in frosty Russia, where they subsequently died. Conrad was then raised from twelve by his kindly uncle, who had him tutored in Latin, Greek, geography, and such. Young Joseph was an impatient student who vowed to sail the world and see Africa. His uncle approved of him becoming a seaman, as it would help him avoid being pressed into the Russian service. He sailed with the French, was a smuggler and gunrunner, and tried to kill himself rather than face a gambling debt he could not pay. He later joined the British merchant service, where he changed his name to Joseph Conrad. Plagued with depression and gout, he steered a paddle steamboat down the Congo for the Belgians and saw firsthand what the colonial powers were doing away from the judgmental prying eyes of "civilization." This novel is disturbing and haunting and controversial well after Conrad's day. The book was published in 1899. In 1975, Chinua Achebe, the noted

Nigerian novelist and educator, gave a lecture at the University of Massachusetts called "An Image of Africa: Racism in Conrad's *Heart of Darkness*" in which he called Conrad "a thoroughgoing racist." Achebe says Conrad is a good writer, but "Although he's writing good sentences, he's also writing about a people, and their life. And he says about these people that they are rudimentary souls. . . . The Africans are the rudimentaries, and then on top are the good whites. Now I don't accept that, as a basis for . . . as a basis for anything." You make up your own mind. The trip down the river to find unhinged corporate despot and jungle kingpin Mr. Kurtz is unique. You will remember Conrad's evocation of lonely madness.

### The Feverhead

Unfortunately your letter crossed with mine.
—Wolfgang Bauer (1941–2005)

{ Hilariously absurd convoluted novel about something or nothing. }

Bauer was an Austrian playwright and a young one. At twenty, he had his first play, *Der Schweinetransport*, or *The Pig Transport*, produced. Bauer drank like a fish and smoked like a wildfire and wrote loads of plays. It is he who coined the term *Theater of the Absurd*. Bauer deals in the surreal and makes little to no effort to help you along. His first hit was *Magic Afternoon*, the tale of bored kids who go wild with violence to alleviate their boredom. The conservative Austrians were not loving him and labeled him an *enfant terrible* and later an experimental playwright. Bauer would have none of it and did his own thing. *The Feverhead* is his only novel. Good luck. By the way, it is laugh-out-loud funny.

## The Adventures
## and Misadventures of Maqroll

When I'm on land, I suffer a kind of restlessness, a frustrating sense of limitation verging on asphyxia. It disappears, though, as soon as I walk up the gangplank of the ship that will take me on one of those extraordinary voyages where life lies in wait like a hungry she-wolf.
—Álvaro Mutis (1923–2013)

{ *Heart of Darkness* with drinking and ghosts and sex. }

Mutis is surely within the Latin literature tradition, but he loved Proust and Dickens, and his identity is mixed in with his dreams and failures. He imagined the character when he was nineteen and finished the series in his sixties, when it was first published. Mutis was a rich kid who shuttled between Belgium and his grandfather's plantation. He was a salesman of TV shows for Hollywood studios and did the voiceover for *The Untouchables* for all of Latin America. He spent years of his life working as the PR guy for Colombian Standard Oil, riding up rivers and ending up in Mexico where, over the misallotment of funds he claims he was using to help friends in danger from Rojas Pinilla's military dictatorship, he was chucked in jail for more than a year. This, Mutis claimed, was the most important chapter of his life: "And there is one thing you learn in prison, and I passed it on to Maqroll, and that is you don't judge, you don't say, that guy committed a terrible crime against his family, so I can't be his friend. No, in a place like that one coexists. The judging is done by the judges on the outside."

## Perfume:
### The Story of a Murderer

He who ruled scent ruled the hearts of men.
—Patrick Süskind (1949–)

{ Super-creepy, demented perfumer wreaks havoc and homicide in Romantic eighteenth-century France. }

Süskind is an odd sort of genius. He is a playwright, history student, linguist, TV writer, novelist, and would-be musician, but something was wrong with his hands. He moved to Paris, where he was supported by his parents, and studied in France, where he trav-  eled through the perfume-making region gathering material for what would become *Perfume*. His first play, *The Double Bass*, is a monologue by the bass player, who is an ancillary player in the orchestra and in his own life. It was rejected for publication a bunch of times until it became a hit play. He then wrote *Perfume*, which was a worldwide smash bestseller and a strenuously medio- cre movie. He started winning awards and just as quickly reject- ing them. He went on to collaborate on two popular German TV shows but has not published a book in years. Personal and always an outsider, Süskind is funny and horrid and poignant.

### The Manuscript Found in Saragossa

It is not science which leads to unbelief but rather ignorance. The ignorant man thinks he understands something provided that he sees it every day. The natural
philosopher walks amid enigmas, always striving to
understand and always half-understanding. He learns
to believe what he does not understand, and that is a
step on the road to faith.
—Jan Potocki (1761–1815)

{ Hanged man spins a web of overlapping tales }
{ of sex and magic. }

The themes in *Saragossa* reflect Potocki's own ceaseless inquisitive-
ness. Sex, magic, revolution, secret societies, philosophy, and the
supernatural. Count Potocki was raised wealthy and learned eight
languages, traveled the world, and studied everyone and everywhere he went. He met and hired Osman, his valet, in Turkey
and began wearing a fez. Potocki sailed with the Knights of Malta
against the Barbary pirates and led expeditions for Tsar Alexander. A Freemason and cohort of the occultist Cagliostro, he was
the first Polish person to fly in a balloon, where he was joined
by Osman and his dog Lulu. Purported to have helped start the
French Revolution while he was frequenting the salons and secret
places in Paris. He married twice; the mother of his second wife,
Princess Julia Lubomirska, founded the Łańcut vodka distillery,
which is still distilling. He suffered from melancholia, which we
call depression. He split for his castle in Poland. Convinced he
was a werewolf, he had for years been filing a silver knob shaped
like a strawberry on top of a sugar bowl his mother had given him
into a bullet. He had the bullet blessed by the castle priest and
shot himself in the head. It is exhausting simply reading about his

adventurous world. His life is as unbelievable and outrageous as this fabulous testament to his deep knowledge and crazed imagination.

## Chéri

Curious how people can go on doing
the same thing day after day!
—Colette (1873–1954)

{ In sexy Belle Époque Paris, a wise, aging courtesan and a young louche rake find sex, love, and *bien sûr* plenty of misery. }

Colette's life is a novel. In fact, she wrote many novels about her amazing life. From the nineteenth century to the age of television, Colette got it on and got it done. She is the antithesis of her famous line: "People who are perfectly sane and happy don't make good literature, alas." She is the first

Woman to be given a state funeral in France. She discovered Audrey Hepburn and put her in *Gigi*. She turned her husband's estate into a hospital in WWI and was awarded a Chevalier of the Légion d'honneur. She performed in music halls and did a scandalous act that had girl-girl kissing, which caused a riot that the police had to quell. Colette helped Jews during WWII and hid her Jewish husband in the attic. She was a noted bisexual, had an affair with her stepson, wrote an opera with Ravel, and was buried with honors amongst the geniuses at Père Lachaise Cemetery. She wrote spicy stories about people who had spicy sex, something she was a spicy expert on. Colette lived long enough to attend a documentary of her own life, where she quipped, "What a wonderful life I've had." We should all experience the scope of love and lusts and war that Colette endured and persevered through. But we don't have the energy.

## Nightwood

And must I,
perchance, like careful writers, guard myself
against the conclusions of my readers?
—Djuna Barnes (1892–1982)

{ You bloody tell me. }

Djuna Barnes's lifetime spans the twentieth century. Born in the 1890s to decidedly weird parents and a grandmother, she is the ultimate bohemian. Wald, her father, believed in free love and polygamy. Djuna had to work to help her family make ends meet. They also abused her sexually. She split to Greenwich Village to study art. She walked into the offices of the *Brooklyn Eagle* and said, "I can draw and write, and you'd be a fool not to hire me." They made her a reporter. Djuna did first-person reporting, features, news stories, interviews, theatrical reviews, and her own illustrations for every paper in New York. In 1914, she did an article with photographs for the *New York World* magazine called "How It Feels to Be Forcibly Fed" when lots of Women suffragettes were on hunger strikes and were being force-fed. Waterboarding, anyone? She moved to Paris and interviewed James Joyce; she wrote plays, had affairs with men and Women; she was the life of the biggest party in that most amazing of places, Paris, during the 1920s, of which Gertrude Stein said, "Paris was the place that suited us who were to create the twentieth century art and literature." Djuna Barnes wrote *Nightwood* after breaking up with the American sculptor Thelma Wood. She was staying out in the country at a house the residents called "Hangover Hall" that was being rented by famous art patron Peggy Guggenheim. She finished the book, and the poet Emily Coleman gave it to T. S. Eliot, the eminent poet and editor who was running Faber and Faber. He championed the book and wrote the foreword, but it was never a hit. She was forced back to New York, where she lived for another forty years, drinking and writing her revenge play about her family, *The Antiphon*.

# SMARTEST BOOK
# BASEBALL TEAM III
# All-Time Controversial Team

### Owner: GEORGE STEINBRENNER (1930–2010)

Steinbrenner was convicted of perjury and was fined and suspended. He was the most meddlesome owner of all time, second-guessed his managers, coaches, players, and the league. He hired and fired his perennial manager and sparring partner Billy Martin five times. Did everything but put on a uniform and run onto the field. He had winning teams but made paying the most for a team the standard, driving the small markets to distraction. No right-thinking human would root for him. That means you, Yankee fans.

### Manager: JOHN JOSEPH McGRAW (1873–1934)

Muggsy was an asshole. To be fair, he lost his family to epidemics and his first wife to a ruptured appendix. He grew up rough and unloved. He did not seek out love later, especially from fans or the league. He cheated and baited umpires and regularly consorted with gamblers. As a player, he was the dirtiest in the league in a time when baseball was never more violent. Grabbing opposing players' belts to keep them from running, stamping on umpires' feet, swearing at the fans. As a manager, he screamed at players, fans, league officials, and had a special hatred for umpires and they for him. When he retired, his last act was to file a complaint with the league about a decision. "The main thing," he said, "is to win." Ten pennants in three decades. A zillion enemies. Tellingly, after his death, his wife found a list of black players he had wanted on his team.

### Third Base Coach: ALFRED "BILLY" MARTIN (1928–1989)

Billy Martin was a country-music-loving maniac and manager of the Yankees five different times. Made every team win. Made every player leery. Made every reporter scared. He once rabbit-punched his own pitcher while managing the A's. Died drunk in his pickup truck on an icy road. We think.

### Catcher: THURMAN MUNSON (1947–1979)

Mustachioed and obstreperous, Munson was a main feature of the Bronx Zoo Yankees of the '70s. He played old-time baseball, blocking the plate and spitting. The Yankees did not want him to fly his private plane, but he did anyway. He crashed. He is shouting "horseshit" from heaven.

### First Base: HAL CHASE (1883–1947)

Chase was a tall, good-looking, talented hitter and a great fielder, but he spent all his time cheating and thinking of ways to make money doing it. He was allowed to stick around for years and went from team to team as a cancer. He was especially vile in his appraisal of honest players. He knew about the gamblers' fix in the

1919 World Series and was finally chucked out when he was about done. He was unrepentant. A real black spot on the game. Even counting the owners.

### Backup First Base: STEVE GARVEY (1948–)

Garvey had a junior high school named after him while he was active. No other player has enjoyed that honor. Handsome and Mr. All-American. Later turned out he had babies with more than eight Women, most of whom he was not married to. So the junior high came in handy.

### Second Base: ROGERS HORNSBY SR. (1896–1963)

Hornsby refused to go to the movies 'cause it would hurt his batting eye. Which is bad enough, but he was also a verified racist and hated by teammates and owners alike. Batted .400 three times, managed several teams, and was a supremely honest announcer, as he would openly say whom he did not like. Impossible man. Great hitter.

### Shortstop: LEO DUROCHER (1905–1991)

When Durocher was a rookie on the Murderers' Row Yankees, Ruth accused him of stealing his watch. He went on to the Gas House Gang Cardinals of the Depression, and on that team of miscreants was so abusive he earned his nickname "The Lip." Suspended for consorting with criminals. He chased broads and traveled with several trunks of tailor-made clothes. A real old-fashioned loudmouth. "Nice guys finish last" is his baseball epitaph. He gave Willie Mays his chance and put down a racist insurrection when he managed Brooklyn. He did not finish last.

### Right Field: REGGIE JACKSON (1946–)

Reggie had his own candy bar—the "Reggie" bar—hit three consecutive home runs on three pitches in the 1977 World Series, and was a great slugger but holds the record for striking out. He called himself "the straw that stirs the drink" and his manager Billy Martin called him "a born liar." Interfered wildly and hipped a ball into the outfield and got away with it in the 1978 series. It took years for baseball to let him even hang around after he retired.

### Center Field: TY COBB (1886–1961)

"The Georgia Peach" was a sociopath with uncontrollable anger issues who regularly beat up teammates, fans, and black people. Carried a gun and supposedly sharpened his spikes so he could cut players when stealing. Liked to drag bunt down the first base line so he could spike pitchers. The one player we can all agree was ferocious. "[Baseball] is no pink tea, and mollycoddles had better stay out," said Ty. Truly a bad apple. Definitely a bad peach.

### Left Field: BARRY BONDS (1964–)

Go ahead and boo and sneer, and jeer and yelp, and whine and wheedle. He could drive a ball anyone else in history would have hit foul for a screaming line drive home run and then stand back and marvel at his creation like Rembrandt watching his masterpiece dry. Best hitter ever. Most controversial player ever. Well, he did what he was asked to do. In twenty years, history will bear *The Smartest Book* out.

## Utility: PETE ROSE (1941–)

He will always be Charlie Hustle. But because he was also a gambler, he is banned for life. Unspeakable hairdo. Total winner.

## PITCHERS

### EARLY WYNN (1920–1999)

Wynn threw at guys' heads when they did not wear helmets. Someone said to him, "You'd put your own grandmother on her ass if she tried to dig in against you." Early responded, "Grandma was a pretty good hitter."

### BOB GIBSON (1935–)

Not only would Gibson not speak with the players on the opposing team, he would not speak to his own teammates on the days he started. Played for a time on the Harlem Globetrotters barnstorming team. Hated it because they clowned and didn't try to win.

### CARL MAYS (1891–1971)

Mays threw sidearm and also at guys' heads. Playing the Indians, Ray Chapman was up and crowding the plate. Mays unleashed one and hit Chapman on the temple. The ball made a such a loud noise Mays thought it hit the bat, and it came back so hard he fielded it and threw to first. Chapman was unconscious and later died. The only fatality caused on the field in Major League history. Mays did not show remorse.

## RELIEVERS

## RICHARD "GOOSE" GOSSAGE (1951–)

Goose Gossage threw hard. Up and in, baby. Duck or be killed.

## RYNE DUREN (1929–2011)

Wore giant Coke-bottle-lens glasses. Threw as fast as hell. Would come out of the bullpen and throw the first warm-up pitch over the catchers' head. Hitters hated him. Drank like an alcoholic fish. Gave an umpire the choke sign during the World Series on TV. Got sober but left a wild legend.

### Designated Hitter (1973–)

Hate the designated hitter and interleague play, ads on the video screens, crappy loud music, and John Kruk on ESPN. Oh, and jet flyovers.

# MUSIC II
# Glam

Glam rock is the most underrated and shallowest of all rock genres. Possibly the goodest. Folk rock is a bit serious, country rock more than a bit rednecky, progressive rock is simply way too top-heavy with elves, and hard rock has an excessive amount of Jethro Tull and not enough Aerosmith. Glam brought for one shining hour men in feather boas and makeup swanning around making twelve-year-olds scream.

## ELECTRIC WARRIOR
### T. Rex, 1971

That is what rock is supposed to be. Marc Bolan of T. Rex delivers the short sexy warlock stuff right to the edge of the enchanted guitar forest for you to wonder on. Mr. Bolan had a bad car wreck and went to meet the fairies way too early, but he is undeniably what makes glam tick. He is a boy who wants a girl, but he also wants to write poetry naked in a forest being chased by nymphs. Trippy flying saucers, cloaks full of eagles, sexy  vampire bites, dangerously exciting gong banging—it is all there, like a romantic novel with drums. Produced by the acute Tony Visconti, who went on to collaborate on thirteen albums with

Bowie, the sound is scaled down and the mood is get me-some-mescaline-and-mascara, I-need-a-hug-on-the-fur-carpet. Wear a giant hat while you do your nails and listen, then throw the file down and rock out. By the way, we don't dance, we dahnce.

## TRANSFORMER
### Lou Reed, 1972

Lou Reed was given electroshock therapy as a teenager to quell his homosexual impulses. His parents did this, as parents so often do, for the child's own good. Lou Reed found himself in New York after college and met John Cale, the classically trained multi-instrumentalist. Sterling Morrison was an old school friend of Reed, and Moe Tucker, the lady drummer, was their buddies' sister. She played standing up, and the weirdest art band of all time was formed. When Paul Morrissey, the director who worked with Andy Warhol, saw them at the perfectly named Café Bizarre playing songs about drugs and kinky sex to a room full of tourists, it was game on. The Velvet Underground is the most famous band that never sold any records. Though it has been said and attributed to Brian Eno that everyone who bought an album started a band. Lou Reed brought the avant-garde to rock as well as the underground of heroin, hustlers, and homosexuality. *Transformer* has four Velvet Underground songs on it, which informs its tough, startling, fluid sexual sensibility. Bowie and Mick Ronson, the guitarist and producer, tried like mad to serve Lou to the male-dominated rock public, and "Walk on the Wild Side," a semi-rapped, midnight jam about drag queens, male hustlers, and fellatio references, was a solid hit and is still shocking. But Lou Reed was a sensitive poet type, and his raw flame of honesty, along with the drone, pop, and fuzz, wasn't meant for mainstream. *Transformer* has rock 'n' roll and art and sadness and all manner of ambiguity. "Perfect Day" is a love song or an ironic put-down or both. Singular in his bold vision and poetry, Lou Reed is a fearless master and drugged-up lunatic. America never wants to reveal its complex underbelly, but that is precisely why we are at all interesting. Lou Reed gives poetry to the hidden class. Lou Reed is your detached, hip, jaded friend taking you on a tour of tenements full of burning mattresses and mad love for life. Light up a fag. Any kind.

# WOMEN WITH
# A CAPITAL *W*

History is a series of lies written by icky white guys who beat their maids. That is why it is so often about how great icky white guys are. We attempt to make this book smarter by including Women who made the world better. They are strong, vital, and fabulous because they had to be.

### FLORYNCE KENNEDY (1916–2000)

If men could get pregnant, abortion would be a sacrament.
—Florynce Kennedy

Grass-roots organizing is like climbing into bed with a malaria patient in order to show how much you love him or her, then catching malaria yourself. I say if you want to kill poverty, go to Wall Street and kick—or disrupt.
—Florynce Kennedy

Florynce Kennedy was an American treasure civil rights hero. She wore a cowboy hat and pink sunglasses and took no prisoners. Hilarious, contentious, and bigger-than-life. From organizing a boycott of a Coca-Cola plant in the '30s for not hiring black drivers to being a lawyer for the Black Panthers, antiwar activist,

abortion champion, and a founding
member of the National Organization for Women, she never took no
for an answer.

As a lawyer, she helped defend
the Black Panthers against charges
of conspiring to blow up stores
and triumphed. It was the longest
political trial in the history of New
York. Try this on, groove kittens:
she sued the record companies for
jazz giants Billie Holiday's and

Charlie Parker's back royalties and won.

Daughter of a Pullman porter, she graduated from Columbia
Law School in 1951, just one of eight Women that year and only
the second black Woman allowed to do so. She had confronted
the dean in 1948 on whether she was being denied admission
because she was black, and the dean told her no, it was because
she was a Woman. Go figure.

She sued the Catholic Church for having tax-exempt status
and spending money on anti-abortion campaigns. She organized a
group to sue the state of New York over their strict abortion laws.
New York liberalized them. But law was too corrupt, and the
system too stodgy for her. She wrote in her memoir *Color Me Flo:
My Hard Life and Good Times*, "Handling the Holiday and Parker
estates taught me more than I was really ready for about government and business delinquency and the hostility and helplessness
of the courts. Not only was I not earning a decent living, there
began to be a serious question in my mind whether practicing law
could ever be an effective means of changing society or even of
simple resistance to oppression."

Her activism was vital in matters of race, war, and Women's
rights. She spoke and wrote, picketed, organized, and galvanized
all through the decades. She brought groups together. Florynce

founded the Feminist Party in 1971. How is that for feminist? They immediately threw their support to that other icon, the first black female member of Congress Shirley Chisholm, who was running against Richard Nixon for president.

Florynce Kennedy fought for the poor and for unity between gender and races. That may be why she is not included in many history books. Gloria Steinem said, "She understood what Emma Goldman understood: there has to be laughter and fun at the revolution, or it isn't a revolution." As Florynce described herself, "I'm just a loud-mouthed middle-aged colored lady with a fused spine and three feet of intestines missing, and a lot of people think I'm crazy. Maybe you do, too, but I never stop to wonder why I'm not like other people. The mystery to me is why more people aren't like me."

If only, Ms. Kennedy. Most people wearing cowboy hats don't have the cojones to wear pink shades and speak truth to power.

## ADA LOVELACE (1815–1852)

> The Analytical Engine weaves algebraic patterns, just
> as the Jacquard loom weaves flowers and leaves.
> —Ada Lovelace

An enchantress of numbers, Ada Lovelace was the first computer programmer, a hundred years before the computer. Sly.

Ada Lovelace was the only legitimate child of the famous poet Lord Byron. Yes, that Lord Byron, the debauched, drinky bisexual member of Parliament and adventurer, the one described by one of his lovers as "Mad, bad, and dangerous to know." His wife, Annabella, a calculating Woman whom Byron called the "Mathematical Medea," thought he was deranged and split the scene. They never saw him again. Her mother forbade his mention, and they lived in the country. But Ada always kept a place in her heart for Byron and was buried next to him. She thought of herself as a poetical scientist.

Ada was quite ill as a child; she spent a whole year in bed with the measles. The staunch Annabella was determined that Ada should not be the insane maniac her father was and made her lie still for hours at a time to learn self-control. Anne also brought in tutors of math and science for the same reason—to drive away the fiery moods—and Ada was an adept pupil from early on. Her teachers were eclectic and a who's who of free thinkers from the age: William Frend, a social reformer; William King, the family's doctor; and Mary Somerville, a Scottish astronomer and mathematician. Mary Somerville was a hit in 1831 when she published *The Mechanism of the Heavens*, a translation of the five-volume *Mécanique Céleste* by Pierre Simon Laplace. She was published by the fantastically named Society for the Diffusion of Useful Knowledge (indeed). She was also one of the first Women to be admitted into the Royal Astronomical Society and has a crater on the moon named after her. But back to young Ada.

Ada was obsessed with machines as a child, designing boats, inventing a steam-powered flying machine, and even writing and illustrating a book called *Flyology*. As a teen, she had an affair with her shorthand tutor and had her coming-out in society. The tutor was fired, and Ada was given the nineteenth-century cure for having a healthy libido: horseback riding. At eighteen, she attended a soirée where the mathematician Charles Babbage was showing his Difference Engine, an advanced calculating machine. She immediately dug it and struck up a working relationship with him.

In the meantime, she married and had three kids. Her husband became the Earl of Lovelace, which gave her her awesome name. She eventually reconnected with Mr. Babbage while he was working on his Analytical Engine, a newer, more complicated animal. This is where the story really heats up. Babbage gave a talk on his engine in Turin, and Luigi Menabrea, a mathematician who later became prime minister of Italy, wrote up the speech in French. How sexy is this story so far? Our Ada then translated and added her own notes. The machine used punch cards, but Ada saw much more than calculating potential—she saw the poetic potential. "Again, it [the Analytical Engine] might act upon other things besides number, were objects found whose mutual fundamental relations could be expressed by those of the abstract science of operations . . . Supposing, for instance, that the fundamental relations of pitched sounds in the science of harmony and of musical composition were susceptible of such expression and adaptations, the engine might compose elaborate and scientific pieces of music of any degree of complexity or extent."

Ada was right, of course, and the notes were wholly her own. She died quite young but is rightly recognized as a visionary in the field of computing and mathematics. Now there is an Ada Lovelace Day, something Mr. Jobs will never get.

## WILMA MANKILLER (1945–2010)

I've run into more discrimination as a woman
than as an Indian.
—Wilma Mankiller

Prior to my election, young Cherokee girls would never have
thought that they might grow up and become chief.
—Wilma Mankiller

Wilma Mankiller has the most fearsome name in this book. She was a Cherokee activist, educator, author; the first Woman ever elected chief by any major American tribe; and hands-down super hardcore.

Born to a family of eleven in Oklahoma, her great-grandfather had been part of the Trail of Tears, the forced relocation of the Cherokee tribe from the Carolinas and Georgia in the 1830s. Her family had been given a depressing tract of ground called Mankiller Flats.

The family eventually ended up in San Francisco, where the government had promised her father a job. They found out they were stuck in crappy public housing in the sleazy Tenderloin district. The shock was a strain she called her own "trail of tears," but she met and married a man and had two daughters. It was the Indian occupation of Alcatraz in 1969 that changed her life. The occupiers claimed the island "in the name of Indians of All Tribes"; they were seeking to call attention to the horrible treatment of Indians by the U.S. government. Wilma started visiting and raising money. She shuttled to the Indian Center that was the command post during the nineteen-month protest.

She wrote that she gained a sense of pride during the Alcatraz occupation: "It changed me forever. Throughout the Alcatraz experience and afterward, I met so many people from other tribes who had a major and enduring effect on me. They changed how I perceived myself as a woman and as a Cherokee." Justine Buckskin, who worked at the center, was helpful to her; she "extended a hand to me at a time I really needed it. So, when I think about women's rights organizations, I think about women extending a hand to other women."

Ms. Mankiller moved back to Oklahoma and took up the cause. She took an entry-level position with the Cherokee Tribe leading campaigns for new health and school programs, like Head Start. Wilma got in a horrible head-on collision and suffered terrible injuries, but she persisted. She got a job as economic stimulus coordinator for the Cherokee Nation, emphasizing community self-help. She founded the community development department of the Cherokee Nation and, as its director, helped develop rural water systems and rehabilitated housing. She was working hard and all the while going to college, so the tribe's principal chief,

Ross Swimmer, selected her as his running mate in his reelection campaign in 1983. Their victory made her the first Woman to become deputy chief of the Cherokee Nation. Along the way she met feminist icon Gloria Steinem and they became friends. Ms. Steinem got married at her house.

She ran for chief after succeeding Ross Swimmer and won her second term with 83 percent of the vote. She had loads of health issues and died early of cancer but not before receiving a Presidential Medal of Freedom from President Clinton.

Nothing could stop her. Not divorce, poverty, illness, or loss.

## PETRA HERRERA (c. 1875–c. 1942)

One of the thousands of Women who fought in the Mexican Revolution, Ms. Herrera fought in men's clothes, led a male unit to victory, and when she didn't get the credit, she put on Women's clothes and led an all-female unit into battle.

Whole villages were swept up by revolutionaries Pancho Villa and Zapata's rolling army, taking Women and children along with them. Often not of their own will or for their own good. They foraged and cooked as they went, and one reporter described the revolutionary Carranza's camp as appearing like "an immense picnic."

The Women who fought in the Mexican Revolution were known as *soldaderas,* and during the chaos of the revolution, they faced terrible abuse and inhuman conditions. Petra, disguised as a man with the name "Pedro Herrera," established herself as a leader and also was good at blowing up bridges. She was there to take names. Eventually, she revealed her gender by wearing braids and became a captain in the rebel army. Villa loved his own reputation as a ladies' man and would not allow *soldaderas* into his elite cavalry unit the Dorados, or "Golden Ones."

In May of 1914, Villa attacked the bastion at Torreón with his force of men and four hundred Women soldiers, with Herrera at the front. She performed exceptionally, and one Villista recalled, "She was the one who took Torreón, she turned off the lights when they entered the city." Villa gave her no special honors, so she split and formed an all-Women brigade where no men were allowed to be in camp after dark. If men were found around, she personally shot at them. That is maintaining discipline.

After the war, she requested a general's rank but did not get it. Instead, they made her a colonel and had her army disbanded. Her end came when, as a rebel spy, she was shot by drunks or hit mob-style, depending on whom you believe, while tending bar.

She died as she lived, feisty and independent.


## YURI KOCHIYAMA (1921–2014)

When I grow up I wanna be just like Yuri Kochiyama.
—The Blue Scholars

White people like Bush, they want to do away
with everyone but themselves.
—Yuri Kochiyama

Activist, organizer, and civil rights champion Mary Yuriko Nakahara was born in San Pedro, California, to Japanese immigrant parents. Her father was arrested for being Japanese right after Pearl Harbor and died of medical inattention.

This is how she remembered that time and her father: "He was in the fishing business. That's why it hit all fishermen, because they knew then that the fishermen knew the waters, and if the Japanese ships got close enough, would the Japanese fishermen in America help the Japanese? But actually, I tell you, the Japanese Americans and even the Isseis, first generation, who could not become Americans, they were so American. And yet, the hysteria about the suspicion of Japanese people was very, very strong."

A month after her dad died in jail, she and her family were "evacuated" to Camp Jerome in Arkansas. Understand, 120,000 Japanese Americans were sent to prison during WWII for being Asian and scary.

She moved to New York City after the war and married Bill Kochiyama. He had served in the all–Japanese American 442nd combat unit of the U.S. Army. He was a decorated soldier who fought for America; the same country imprisoned her. We are sure there is irony here, but it is hard to ascertain.

They moved to a housing project in Harlem, and their crib became the meeting place for all the activist groups, from the black and Puerto Rican communities to the Freedom Riders, who were getting beaten for trying to ride buses across state lines while ethnic.

The kids went to Harlem Freedom School. Yuri and eldest son Billy were arrested while protesting for jobs for blacks and Puerto Ricans in the construction of the Downstate Medical Center in Brooklyn. That's how she came to be friends with Malcolm X. She was being arraigned at a courthouse in Brooklyn when she got to meet him and get in his face.

She said, "I admire what you're doing, but I disagree with some of your thoughts."

"And what don't you agree with?" Malcolm X replied.

"Your harsh stand on integration."

Eventually, Malcolm left the Nation of Islam and formed the Organization for Afro-American Unity, which she joined. She invited him to her apartment to meet some atom bomb survivors from the Hiroshima-Nagasaki World Peace Mission; they wanted to meet him more than any other American. Yuri wasn't sure he would come, but he did. Just him and a bodyguard. They spoke of the scars of war and racism.

He sent her and her husband postcards from his trip to Africa, including this one: "Still trying to travel and broaden my scope, since I've learned what a mess can be made by narrow-minded people. Bro. Malcolm X."

Yuri was there when he was assassinated and held him in her arms, a picture that was immortalized in *Life* magazine. She continued her work after his death and joined the Republic of New Africa, the Puerto Rican Young Lords Party, and Asian Americans for Action. She was for building "bridges, not walls."

It took years, but the U.S. government finally apologized for the policy of imprisoning Japanese Americans during the war, and in 1988 the Civil Liberties Act was signed; with the apology came $20,000 in restitution for each living survivor of the camps.

Yuri carried on speaking, organizing, and agitating for freedom and self-determination into her nineties.

# POETRY V
## Sappho
### (610–580 BC)

Sappho exists in fragments and recollections. The learned Alexandrians of ancient times adored her. She comes from the island that gives its name to Women in love. Sappho—the dream and ideal; she is all about love, and the most famous purported lesbian of antiquity. We have only a small part of her poetry, some recalled and some from scrolls, and so we may only imagine the breadth of her gift. She is randy and lovely and eternal. Jove is Jupiter, aka the Greek god Zeus, the king of the gods. Venus is the Greek Aphrodite, the goddess of love. But keep in mind, she loved Mars, the god of war.

### A Hymn to Venus

O Venus, beauty of the skies,
To whom a thousand temples rise,
Gaily false in gentle smiles,
Full of love-perplexing wiles,
O goddess, from my heart remove
The wasting cares and pains of love.

If ever thou hast kindly heard
A song in soft distress preferr'd,

Propitious to my tuneful vow,
O gentle goddess, hear me now.
Descend, thou bright immortal guest,
In all thy radiant charms confest.

Thou once did leave almighty Jove,
And all the golden roofs above:
The car thy wanton sparrows drew;
Hovering in air they lightly flew;
As to my bower they winged their way
I saw their quivering pinions play.

The birds dismissed (while you remain),
Bore back their empty car again:
Then you, with looks divinely mild,
In every heavenly feature smil'd,
And ask'd what new complaints I made,
And why I call'd you to my aid?

What frenzy in my bosom raged,
And by what cure to be assuaged?
What gentle youth I would allure,
Whom in my artful toils secure?
Who does thy tender heart subdue?
Tell me, my Sappho, tell me who?

Though now he shuns thy longing arms,
He soon shall court thy slighted charms;
Though now thy offerings he despise,
He soon to thee shall sacrifice;
Though now he freeze, he soon shall burn,
And be thy victim in his turn.

Celestial visitant, once more
Thy needful presence I implore!
In pity come, and ease my grief,
Bring my distempered soul relief,
Favour thy suppliant's hidden fires,
And give me all my heart desires.


### Blame Aphrodite

It's no use
Mother dear, I
can't finish my
weaving
   You may
blame Aphrodite

soft as she is
she has almost
killed me with
love for that boy

# THE WAY BACK II
## Julius Caesar
### (100 BC–44 BC)

Caesar was an opportunist who came late to the game. His was a life of adventure, hardball politics, and terrifying wars. He slayed a million foes and got with every Woman in the Empire and plenty of men, too, if you believe everyone. He borrowed mad amounts  of money, forged alliances, escaped from pirates, dodged murderers, stole insane amounts of booty, wrote books about himself, invented letter writing, had a baby with the wily Queen of Egypt, Cleopatra, wore thigh-high red boots and a red cape and was rubbed out by rivals who thought he had too much power and was riding too high in his pleated brass skirt. And he died as he lived, burning with ambition.

His name is a title—*czar* and *kaiser* are later incantations—and his legacy is scattered wide across our culture: his haircut, his month (July), his salad, the phrase "I came, I saw, I conquered," his rep as a master politician, his bloody murder. We Americans even hold a connection to Caesar in our pockets, as our money has an eagle holding a bunch of arrows. Caesar would easily recognize this emblem (and he would have loved to have had predator drones).

---

### ON FASCES AND EAGLES

A fasces is a bundle of birch rods with an axe or two stuck in. In Rome important magistrates had their underlings, or lictors, carry these as symbols of their power as they proceeded through town. The axes stood for the power of life and death.

The eagle, or *aquila*, was carried by every Roman legion and was a symbol of strength and domination. But America's eagle did it best. Because we say we did.

---

Gaius Julius Caesar was born to an illustrious family who claimed to be descended from the goddess Venus—so there's that insanity. His mother, Aurelia, raised him in a modest apartment in Subura, which is where we get the word *suburb*. His aunt Julia married Marius, a legendary figure in Rome for his feats as a general and as the man who let the poor into the army.

Julius barely made it through his youth without getting the boom lowered. Sulla, Marius's chief rival, spared young Julius only at the pleading of relatives and the Vestal Virgins. It would not be the only time the goddess Fortune favored him. Sulla was wary and said of Caesar, "I see many a Marius in him." He would go on to surpass the greatness predicted.

Caesar served as a young officer in Turkey where, according to rumor, he also served the king as a young boy toy. He won laurels, which he dug, as his hair was already thinning and they helped hide it. He also combed his hair forward to compensate, a style that would become known as a Caesar, which Napoleon later copied.

While sailing to Rhodes, he was captured by pirates. Their chief goal was ransom. While captive, he socialized and read them verses, and when the pirates didn't understand them, he told them they were barbarians, reminding them that when he was free, he would come back and have them executed. By crucifixion.

When the ransom was delivered, he changed his mind and slit their throats first, out of mercy; Caesar didn't shilly-shally.

He joined up with Rome's most famous general, Pompey the Great. Pompey married Caesar's daughter, making Caesar Pompey's father-in-law even though he was younger. Creepy and useful. Rich Women in Rome were often married and divorced for social movement. Caesar and Pompey brought in Crassus, who was wildly rich, and formed the first Triumvirate.

Caesar needed gravity, a great deed, something to make people stop thinking he was a jumped-up tart with a receding hairline. Gaul, or France, was a plum with advanced agriculture, great goods, and hundreds of sophisticated tribes of people, though like any dominant culture, the Romans thought anyone foreign was a barbarian. He sure enough  brought home the big baguette. Hard-assing the locals and looting everything, he built a fortune in France. All the while he dictated his exploits, sometimes on horseback, to secretaries. This book survives as *The Gallic Wars*; it is mostly about how great he is.

---

### THE VESTAL VIRGINS

The Vestal Virgins had the distinction of being the only Women in Rome who were not completely controlled by their fathers. They strode around town awesomely proceeded by lictors carrying fasces. Messing with the Virgins meant instant death; they were noble-born girls who were chosen for their physical perfection to perform religious duties and keep all the wills of Rome because they were incorruptible. Although their lives were prescribed by men, they had more autonomy than any Women in Rome.

---

Caesar's relations with his troops are key in his tremendous military success. On campaign they were "comrades" and always got huge bonuses. He occasionally let the troops sack a place and rape and pillage, to keep them happy. He knew names, ate camp food, and marched with the men. They knew he chased Women and that he had random epileptic attacks; for that they loved him.

After a great victory against the Gaul armies, he turned his army back to Rome, but the Senate forbade him to come back in triumph. He was a fame whore now and knew what had to be done. He crossed the River Rubicon with the whole force.

"The die is cast," said he. Caesar loved gambling; this time he rolled the bones for the whole focaccia: Rome and the Empire.

---

### THE TRIUMPH

The Roman triumph was in effect a giant parade/rally/ banquet meets religious festival. Legions sang bawdy songs about how Julius was man to every wife and wife to every man. But the lines that really paint a picture is this tasty lyric: "Romans, watch your wives, see the bald adulter- er's back home, You fucked away in Gaul the gold you borrowed here in Rome." Girls strewing flowers, cap- tives in chains, exotic wild animals from captured lands, wagons full of gold, statues, treasure, giant paintings on floats depicting battles, lists of territories taken and ene- mies slain. This PR sometimes backfired as Cleopatra's half sister, Arsinoe, was forced to march in chains in the African triumph, and she was so young and lovable, the crowd wept. Certainly Cleopatra killed herself in part to be spared marching in submission through Rome as part of the triumph of Augustus (Caesar's adopted nephew and eventual successor).

Rome was always of two minds about Caesar. The populace adored him, but the Senate was never too sure about him. Cicero vilified Caesar's best friend Marc Antony, for which he paid by having his eloquent tongue poked through with a needle.

The Senate decided to deal with Caesar's power grab by throwing yet another Roman civil war led by Pompey, who had a huge army of Romans and client states bankrolled by the Senate. Cato, who hated Caesar for having an affair with his sister, Servilia, and other leading lights were already cocksure of victory. Their tents were laid with ivy and silver plates as they prepared for the victory banquet, but Caesar was having none of it. He snatched a ridiculously quick victory against the huge force, and Pompey was forced to don a disguise and escape to Alexandria.

Caesar gave chase all the way to Egypt, but the Egyptians—thinking they were doing him a solid—killed Pompey and presented Caesar with the head. Caesar wept and was revolted because he had loved Pompey but was probably doing a secret victory dance as he was spared having to kill his old partner and former son-in-law.

While in Alexandria, Caesar received another present—a laundry bag holding a nubile young lady. Specifically, the daughter of the dead king and wife and sister of the new king, Ptolemy. This would be the canny, seductive, smart as a whip, and ruthless-as-the-century-she-was-born-in Cleopatra. She needed and wanted Rome on her side and wasted no time in making this happen with Caesar.

War broke out and Caesar, with his small force, set fire to the Egyptian fleet. The fire spread and Caesar, recognizing a partner with ambitions as outsized as his, moved his chips all in and placed Cleopatra on the throne. Though first he had to clear out some space. Setting fire to the Egyptian fleet moved things along nicely. Sadly, the fire burned part of the library at Alexandria, the most famous repository of knowledge, books, inventions, artwork, and halls of learning in the ancient world. But a small price to pay for getting the throne for your girlfriend.

They took an intimate, monthlong honeymoon cruise down the Nile. No matter that he was technically still married back in Rome. Caesar grooved on the swirling incense and the scantily clad dancing girls, the endless finery, and the strange animal gods. In comparison, Rome was so businesslike, as were her gods. Cleopatra bore him a son, Caesarion, and he gave her three legions to guard her new kingdom. With Egypt under control with a new Roman puppet ruler—lover and mother of his son—Caesar left for Turkey to deal with the errant King Pharnaces.

The victory was so swift and decisive, he sent the Senate the message "Vini, vidi, vici": "I came, I saw, I conquered." In the triumph over this kingdom, he had this laconic placard displayed instead of action scenes of his win.

Caesar returned to Rome from his campaigns and threw a bitching party and gave himself four lavish Triumphs, as well as a bonus to everyone in Rome. No wonder the common folks loved him.

Caesar was elected *dictator perpetuo*, which means exactly what you think it does. He forgave his rivals and handed out money from his vast fortune. He made colonials into Roman citizens and—shock, horror—let Gauls into the Senate. Big hairy foreigners that of course spoke Latin and owed him their gig. He was wearing a gold crown now and high red boots; he claimed it was an ancient fashion play. Everyone else thought he was being campy. Cleopatra had been brought over with her son, his son, and was partying with important visitors at his crib outside of town. The month July was named for him. In the Senate plans began in secret to kill him for the good of the state. Because no one can stand a winner in thigh-high red boots.

Cassius and Brutus, the rising young star of the Senate, were the main plotters. They decided to grab him in the Senate and do the deed there. They called their band the Liberators.

At a dinner party the topic came up: What is the best way to die? Which death is best? Caesar jumped in before anyone had digested the question. "Unexpected" was his reply. He was determined to be the sexiest emperor, and he certainly took that cake.

He had every warning about his fate. A soothsayer warned him about going out on March 15, the Ides of March. When the day came, he was called to the Senate and met by a senator, Cimber, who grabbed Caesar and pulled down his tunic. Caesar now knew what was going on. He shouted, "Why, this is violence." Casca raised his dagger, but Caesar caught his arm. Then the Liberators were on him, daggers unsheathed from the leather pouches where they kept their styluses. Caesar tried to fight back but was overwhelmed. He caught sight of Brutus and said, "You too, my son?" A figure of speech. Caesar's favorite mistress was Brutus's mother, Servilia, but it is most likely Brutus was not his son. Just a moralistic, idealistic rich kid who was going to solve Rome's problem in the traditional way: assassination. The Liberators ran into the streets yelling, "Rome is free." But the streets were empty. Finally, some slaves wrapped Caesar up and carried him off, where by all accounts the first recorded autopsy was performed. The doctor declared he had been stabbed twenty-three times, but only the second blow was fatal.

In the name of freedom and the republic, the Liberators had murdered Caesar. But in the end, his death finished the Republic for good. Caesar's dream of total power and empire was his last bequest to his rivals and his friends. At least we still have the eagle.

# SMARTEST BOOK
# BASEBALL TEAM IV
# Roman Emperor Top Nine

### Manager: JULIUS CAESAR (100 BC–44 BC)

When your motto is "I came, I saw, I conquered," you have loads of spirit. Apparently, there is mostly "I" in team. Caesar conquered France and beat all his rivals in a massive civil war. He escaped from pirates as a young man and came back to have them all crucified. He also wrote his own books about how tremendous he was. He invented kicking butt and taking names. He can manage, he just can't handle backstabbing.

### First Base: AUGUSTUS (63 BC–14 AD)

Caesar's adopted nephew Augustus is the once and future dictator of Rome. Though a little short for a first-sacker, he has staunch character and immense guile. He beat Mark Antony, he bested Cleopatra, he immortalized all his accomplishments in marble, and he ran the Empire for sixty years. "He drank little and ate less" was the book on Augustus. Abstemious and controlling, his wife, Livia, was pregnant when he pulled her out of her first marriage so that he could marry her himself. He had his own daughter banished for being a slattern. He always got his way. His reach for an errant throw might get you exiled or executed, so throw well, Roman.

## Second Base: TIBERIUS (42 BC–37 AD)

A studious man and reluctant emperor, Tiberius boned out to Rhodes to study. When he was finally forced to accept the post, he split and went to Capri for ten years. He can pivot and turn two. A durable general and, legend has it, a giant pervert. He can go up the middle and stretch out on the turf. Hide the ball, boys and girls.

## Shortstop: HELIOGABALUS (203–222)

A cross-dressing, pansexual freakazoid, Heliogabalus was high priest of a cult that worshiped a black stone he brought from Syria. Heliogabalus wore a wig, worked as a lady prostitute, and even took a slave as his wife. He will not be bothered by hot shots and liners coming at him. He covers a lot of ground.

## Third Base: MARCUS AURELIUS (121–180)

The hot corner requires some philospohy. Do I come in on a sacrifice bunt? What is the meaning of playing the line? As emperor and a Stoic philospher, Marcus has that covered. Upon his deathbed, he chided the people who wept for him. He is a serious threat to rewrite how we play the game.

## Left Field: HADRIAN (76–138)

Poetic and awesomely gay, Hadrian traveled the length and breadth of the Empire. He built a wall in England to keep the woolly northerners out and built a whole city in Egypt for his boyfriend, Antinous. He also built that amazing dome, the Pantheon. Hadrian covers mad ground in left and has the long arm to throw out guys at the plate.

### Center Field: CONSTANTINE THE GREAT (272–337)

Constantine saw a cross burning in the sky on the battlfield before he kicked Maxentius the tyrant's booty. He made the Empire Christian, made himself sole emperor, and moved the capital to Constantinople in Turkey. Constantine also likely had his wife and son done in. He will hold down center with faith and power. Or you will pay.

### Right Field: NERO (37–68)

Nero was a famous weirdo who killed his mother, two wives, and a stepbrother. He terrorized the streets of Rome with his boy gang. Nero married two male slaves and was wife to one and husband to the other. He can play the far wall as well as anyone. If there is a fire, he will blame the Christians.

### Catcher: CALIGULA (12–41)

This teenage madman can handle balls.

### Pitcher: TRAJAN (53–117)

Trajan was a kick-ass general and bisexual stud muffin. He managed the Empire when it was at its most expansive. Give him the sphere and let him expand the strike zone to the maximum.

# POETRY VI
## François Villon
### (c. 1431–c. 1463)

A scoundrel and thief, François Villon was born poor and adopted by a priest who gave him his last name and an education. He was a rough customer, poised for a career in law or the church, but he killed a priest in a drunken brawl. He split in a hurry, though the priest on his deathbed forgave him. Back in Paris, he wrote "Le Petit Testament." He is said to have finished the poem on Christmas as an alibi for robbing five hundred gold crowns from the local strongbox. His crime  gang was getting hanged, so he hid out, eventually getting a pardon with help from the Duke of Orleans, who was a fan of his work. He carried on robbing and being arrested and composed his greatest piece, the 2,000-plus lines of "Le Testament," which includes "Ballade des Dames du temps jadis" ("The Ballad of Dead Ladies"). Translated by Dante Gabriel Rossetti in the nineteenth century, it works his most famous line "Where are the snows of yester-year?" Villon has been copied and checked by everyone from Bertolt Brecht, Ezra Pound, and Truman Capote to *Catch-22* to *Downton Abbey*. He is an irresistible villain who defied the noose. In real life, he escaped the gallows and ended up heaven knows where. One thing is sure: he, like so many, was an unknown poet in his life and reached immortality in the next world. For a poet like him—part savant, part gangster—it's apropos.

## To Death, of His Lady

Death, of thee do I make my moan,
Who hadst my lady away from me,
Nor wilt assuage thine enmity
Till with her life thou hast mine own;
For since that hour my strength has flown.
Lo! what wrong was her life to thee,
Death?
Two we were, and the heart was one;
Which now being dead, dead I must be,
Or seem alive as lifelessly
As in the choir the painted stone,
Death!

## The Ballad of Dead Ladies

Tell me now in what hidden way is
Lady Flora the lovely Roman?
Where's Hipparchia, and where is Thais,
Neither of them the fairer woman.
Where is Echo, beheld of no man,
Only heard on river and mere,—
She whose beauty was more than human? . . .
But where are the snows of yester-year?

Where's Héloise, the learned nun,
For whose sake Abeillard, I ween,
Lost manhood and put priesthood on?
(From Love he won such dule and teen!)

And where, I pray you, is the Queen
Who willed that Buridan should steer
Sewed in a sack's mouth down the Seine? . . .
But where are the snows of yester-year?

White Queen Blanche, like a queen of lilies,
With a voice like any mermaiden,—
Bertha Broadfoot, Beatrice, Alice,
And Ermengarde the lady of Maine,—
And that good Joan whom Englishmen
At Rouen doom'd and burn'd her there,—
Mother of God, where are they then? . . .
But where are the snows of yester-year?

Nay, never ask this week, fair lord,
Where they are gone, nor yet this year,
Except with this for an overword,—
But where are the snows of yester-year?

# MOVIES III
# Foreign Films

### LA DOLCE VITA
**Federico Fellini, director, 1960**

This film invented foreign films. Marcello Mastroianni is a jaded reporter in this wildly prescient ride through Rome in 1960. Religious mania, aggressive TV crews, the shallowness and bitterness of free sex and glamorous living, the sterility of success, and impending suicide are all examined by the keen eye of Fellini. This movie introduced paparazzi. The film is a series of episodes strung together in the life of our hero. He sails and swings and dallies and gets punched—literally and metaphorically. The costumes and settings are not to be forgotten. Sunglasses indoors at night, bambino. The voluptuous Anita Ekberg does a dance in the Trevi Fountain that is so invigorating it cannot be forgotten. (Evidently, she was cool with being in the freezing cold while they shot; Marcello was freezing and had to drink a bottle of vodka and wear a wetsuit underneath.) *La Dolce Vita* still stings and rings true. Fellini shows you the tragedy of our world of vapidity while making everything look hip and beautiful. Required.

## THE LIVES OF OTHERS
### Florian Henckel von Donnersmarck,
### director, 2006

A film most pertinent in this time of mass eavesdropping and surveillance, *The Lives of Others* is a moving and horrifying look at the police state and the inevitable corruption of those doing the spying. East Germany was a nightmare of oppression. You could be sure you were being watched and listened to all the time. A casual remark might find you disappeared. The rotting corruption and climate of fear led to many suicides and botched escape attempts over the wall as people were desperate to leave the bad food, starving prostitutes, and joyless cafés. Stasi captain Wiesler (Ulrich Mühe) is an undercover agent for the secret police. Looking for evidence of disloyalty to the regime, he bugs the apartment of a playwright and his girlfriend. When he discovers that his boss is having a forced affair with the girlfriend, his motives for spying become personal. Our captain starts to feel sympathetic to the playwright. He begins to protect and intervene in the case. This is not part of the spy plan. Soul-searching, scathing, one sits transfixed as the drama of lying and deceit plays out. To make it all more incredible, Ulrich Mühe was an actor in East Germany, and he was spied on—even by his wife. When asked how he prepared for the role as the spy, he said, "I remembered." You will never forget this movie or move freely through your life without paranoia again. Look behind you. Oh, it's nothing. Keep reading.

## THE CELEBRATION
### Thomas Vinterberg, director, 1998

This was the first Dogme film out of Denmark. In a way, it sparked Denmark's groovy cultural renaissance. Denmark used to be boring but dependable, now they have top chefs, fashion, influential TV shows like *The Killing*, and a new sense of self-confidence. Dogme is a group of filmmakers, including Lars von Trier and the director/nondirector Thomas Vinterberg. The Dogme manifesto states no credit for the director. They wanted to be authentic; no special effects and less Hollywood commercial. This film fits the bill. A well-off family is having a sixtieth birthday party for their dad at the family-owned hotel. During the party the son announces the unspeakable: the father molested him and his sister, who has recently killed herself over the trauma. Everyone goes into denial, and the film takes off from there. This is the opposite of so many Hollywood pictures as it doesn't cute up the subject or back off with jokes. Brutally honest, racist, funny, and real, this film takes on a subject deep and inhuman in a powerful way. Character and plot star. Tough going made better by the skill with which the characters develop.

## THE 400 BLOWS
### François Truffaut, director, 1959

Quintessential French New Wave picture. Antoine Doinel (Jean-Pierre Léaud) is a troubled kid in Paris. His teachers hate him, and his parents are not digging his behavior. The system is stacked against him, as he ends up at reform school where the trouble continues. Shot in the classic French New Wave style (naturalistic, handheld, fly-on-the-wall), this wonderfully honest movie smacks of emotional realism and an improvisational air. Léaud is tremendous as our boy with an old soul buffeted by indifference and judgment from all the adults.

Léaud had his mother take him to audition where Truffaut was blown away by his poise and quiet maturity. He acted like a forty-year-old trapped in a child's body. Truffaut took him to Cannes with the film, and the poet and artist Jean Cocteau proclaimed that Jean-Pierre was going to be a star. And he was right. The film spawned a whole series of semibiographical projects directed by François Truffaut that all star Jean-Pierre as Antoine. A liberating movie of adolescence and an accurate, disquieting, lovely film.

## EYES WITHOUT A FACE
### Georges Franju, director, 1960

The most elegant and riveting horror movie you will ever see. Georges Franju made documentaries about slaughterhouses and military hospitals, and he uses that feel and spooky elements to make this stately black-and-white story painfully claustrophobic. Sometimes you feel as if you can't breathe with the tight, alien atmosphere. The set is oppressive, the soundtrack is oppressive, the dogs barking are oppressive, and the dad is wickedly oppressive.

A mad doctor whose daughter is hideously disfigured in a car wreck sends his minion into Paris to pick up girls so he can remove their faces. Are you with me so far? He is desperate to find one to transplant onto his beloved daughter. He also experiments with dogs that he keeps locked up in a kennel. The incessant barking gives this picture a terrible urgency. The single most excruciating scene is an airless operating room where the doctor surgically and methodically removes a Woman's face—a scene not to be erased or forgotten. Spoiler alert: the doctor does not triumph, but the ending is full of Gallic ambivalence. This is really a movie about Women and power, and Women win. Evil dad doctors lose. This picture will answer the eternal conundrum: Who let the dogs out? Sorry.

## THE SEVENTH SEAL
### Ingmar Bergman, director, 1957

So many riffs have been done on this film for a reason. It is simple and profound and terrible. The austere and iconic Max von
Sydow is a knight returned from the Crusades to a pestilent and
starving Sweden. His face is what movies are about: frosty, lean,
and angular with blue eyes searching his soul and our morality.
He sees nothing but death and dishonesty until he meets some
traveling players. They and their happy family imbue him with
the only sliver of humanity he can find after the horrors he's seen.
It's a play of conscience and darkness told with awe and humor.
The movie is beautifully written and hangs off Max von Sydow's
cheekbones and his penetrating Viking gaze. Ingmar Bergman
takes no budget and makes a fairy tale about heaven and hell and
the plague. Death is a constant purring presence that is playing
the big match with our hero. Who can beat death? This film is
strangely optimistic and everything it is cracked up to be.

## LE SAMOURAÏ
### Jean-Pierre Melville, director, 1967

French directors give good homage. They do for the American
gangster picture what the British groups of the '60s did for rhythm
& blues. *Le Samouraï* is terse and existential. Alain Delon is like
a jungle cat, if a cat smoked and wore a trench coat. He stalks
through the clubs and alleys of Paris eluding the death both he
and we know is coming his way. He barely registers his girlfriend,
and he never eats or sleeps; he is just cool. His room is a cell, and
his world is full of rats—metaphorical gangster rats. No one sleep-
walks through violence like Delon, and no one takes as much
care with every inch of the frame as Jean-Pierre Melville. Gaze in
wonder at the sets. Light a Gitane and keep your gat ready.

# SMARTEST BOOK
# BASEBALL TEAM V
# All-Time British Monarchy
# Baseball Team

### Manager: ELIZABETH I (reign: 1558–1603)

The Virgin Queen spoke six languages, rode on horseback all over England, had her sister executed, attended the premiere of *A Midsummer Night's Dream*, never married so as not to share power, beat the Spanish Armada, and sent Drake around the world. She can manage this team. If you miss a sign, she will have your head lopped off. She has a huge female member.

### Bench Coach: JAMES (reign in England: 1603–1625)

James had the Bible rewritten. He knows the rules.

### First Base: HENRY VIII (reign: 1509–1547)

Huge and athletic, Henry VIII was a great tennis player as well. He stared down the pope and was a frequent killer of his own wives. He holds down first for all England.

## Second Base: ETHELRED II THE UNREADY
### (reign: 979–1013, 1014–1016)

Ethelred's full name says it all. He tried killing the Vikings, then bribing the Vikings. Bad planning or versatile? Certainly flexible. He can go in the hole and turn two.

## Third Base: MARY, QUEEN OF SCOTS
### (reign: 1542–1567)

She was six feet tall. The hot corner is all hers. She was the one who wore a red wig and was waxed by her cousin Elizabeth. She also gave birth to James I, who succeeded Elizabeth, so who had the last laugh? Line drives do not scare her. Nothing scares her.

## Shortstop: EDWARD III THE CONFESSOR
### (reign: 1042–1066)

Frugal and deeply religious, Edward can use faith and divine justice to run down ground balls and argue with the umpires.

## Left Field: CHARLES I (reign: 1625–1649)

Scottish dad, Danish mother, Charles fought and lost a civil war but was such a badass that on the cold day of his execution, he asked for warm clothes. He said, "The season is so sharp as probably may make me shake, which some observers may imagine proceeds from fear. I would have no such imputation." No such imputation given, sir. He can play the wall.

### Center Field: GEORGE VI (reign: 1936–1952)

Diligent and resolute, George stood tall during WWII. Buckingham Palace was bombed nine times, and he never split. He can flag flies. He visited troops all through the war. Father of the longest-reigning monarch, Elizabeth II. He plays center without a hitch or stammer.

### Right Field: GEORGE III (reign: 1760–1820)

He will be great in the garden talking to the birds. George III lost America, but he will win ball games.

### Pitcher: ELIZABETH II (reign: 1952–)

After a million years in the show, Elizabeth has staying power and the crazy fastball.

### Catcher: RICHARD THE LIONHEARTED (reign: 1189–1199)

Richard I was a hot-tempered dude and a cruel-assed Crusader who beat the mighty Saladin. He did get captured, but after being ransomed, he was crowned king of England a second time. He is my field general.

## Relief Pitcher: WILLIAM THE CONQUEROR
### (reign: 1066–1087)

They don't call you The Conqueror unless you are a bona fide badass. They also called him William the Bastard because he was. William I had three horses killed under him at Hastings. He rode waving his helmet so the troops could see he was alive—he can save the game.

## Vendor: HER MAJESTY ELIZABETH,
### the Queen Mother (reign: 1936–1952)

Queen during WWII, Elizabeth took pistol training. Super gay-friendly and drank seventy drinks a week. She'll sell beer and wine in the stands and drink it as well. Passed at 101. Baby, that is hanging tough.

# POETRY VII
# William Shakespeare, aka Willy the Shake
## (1564–1616)

He is impossible to kill. A million bad adaptations cannot pierce the armor around his reputation. No one can deny the majesty of his work. He is the greatest playwright of the English language. Even in this illiterate age of reality TV and the interweb, we all know Hamlet and his dilemma. Macbeth and his terrible crimes. Romeo and Juliet and their mad, doomed love. The truth is, he knew

much about humanity and what makes us human and was able to brilliantly and poetically communicate these deep draughts seemingly with infinite ease and wit. The sonnets are divided into several sets. Some written to a man, some written to "The Dark Lady." We are not about or able to unravel the whys and wherefores here. "The play's the thing," but Shake was also a prolific poet. His wry take on love and his towering way with words are given full play in his poetry. The plays were stepped on, cut, redacted, and rewritten freely by actors and many others. The sonnets are all his and all ours to hold like a precious flower. Just let the master take you there. Pour some mead and hike up your merkin.

## Sonnet 18: Shall I Compare Thee to a Summer's Day?

Shall I compare thee to a summer's day?
Thou art more lovely and more temperate.
Rough winds do shake the darling buds of May, And summer's
    lease hath all too short a date.
Sometime too hot the eye of heaven shines, And often is his
    gold complexion dimmed; And every fair from fair
    sometime declines,
By chance, or nature's changing course, untrimmed; But thy
    eternal summer shall not fade,
Nor lose possession of that fair thou ow'st, Nor shall death brag
    thou wand'rest in his shade,
When in eternal lines to Time thou grow'st.
So long as men can breathe, or eyes can see,
So long lives this, and this gives life to thee.

## Sonnet 151

Love is too young to know what conscience is;
Yet who knows not, conscience is born of love?
Then, gentle cheater, urge not my amiss,
Lest guilty of my faults thy sweet self prove.
For thou betraying me, I do betray
My nobler part to my gross body's treason;
My soul doth tell my body that he may
Triumph in love; flesh stays no farther reason,
But rising at thy name, doth point out thee
As his triumphant prize. Proud of this pride,
He is contented thy poor drudge to be,
To stand in thy affairs, fall by thy side.
No want of conscience hold it that I call
Her "love," for whose dear love I rise and fall.

# MUSIC III
# Punk

Punk was many things, including a reaction to awful music like the hideous elf rock of Yes and the intolerable countrified coke droning of the Eagles, but it was also an art movement spearheaded by low-rent bands in shit clubs. Punk was misunderstood at the time because the American press fixated on the spitting and the safety pins and missed the whole idea that young people hated how boring society had become, loathed the government and the crappy economy, plus the fact that pop music was not getting it done.

## NEVER MIND THE BOLLOCKS
### The Sex Pistols, 1977

Conceived and recorded very quickly and with little to no Sid Vicious, who could not actually play his bass, this album is a snarling, raging, caterwauling triumph. Johnny (then) Rotten barks and yelps and whines and is everything rock needs to rock. Thirty-some odd years down the road, this album, with its opening of marching jackboots, is still snotty. "God Save the Queen" is a hate-packed rant that feels good on every listen. "We mean it, *maaaaaan*." The song "Bodies" says it all: "Fuck this and fuck that." Name another group that made only one album that is still being spoken of. They defined punk and could not sustain because of business and money and drugs and violence. They wrote but one book, but it is a rockin' good time.

## LONDON CALLING
### The Clash, 1979

The Clash had been there at the start of punk and wanted to make an album that had everything but the kitchen sink: rhythm & blues, reggae, ska, lounge, horns, rockabilly, rock 'n' roll, punk, and plenty of anger and dread. And why not? The Sex Pistols were long gone, and punk was morphing into art, techno, industrial, and new wave. The producer was a gifted, drug-taking drunk named Guy Stevens, who brought Chuck Berry to the UK after he was arrested for taking a fourteen-year-old girl across state lines, and started Mott the Hoople and gave them their name. *London Calling*, with its cover art inspired by Elvis's first album, was the title of a book Stevens read in jail. While the first Clash album sounds like machine guns and barking seals, *London Calling* was an attempt to commercialize them and smooth out the punk. The Clash put down a lot of tracks in one take and made the album in a big hurry. It is a sprawling and slightly disorganized record; the hit "Train in Vain" ain't even listed on the album, after a promotional deal fell through. But it has an immediate party feel that is so infectious it covers the mistakes and erratic tempo changes. As Guy Stevens said, "All great rock songs speed up." Light one up before breakfast and stop being so rude and feckless; this record is a call to arms—and shows that pretentious political bands can have fun, too. Dear U2, please take note.

## ROCKET TO RUSSIA
### The Ramones, 1977

Four dysfunctional dudes from New York who loved comic books, sci-fi, baseball, and old-fashioned rock 'n' roll created the greatest art project that rock ever had. The group that defined the look and shred of punk. The Ramones had unity, short buzz-saw songs, the same haircut, leather jackets, ripped jeans, and tennis shoes. The inspired mixture of Beach Boys riffs, drug references, poverty, and nonstop, no solos, maximum rock 'n' roll without the macho bullshit and pretend bluesiness of heavy metal. It is the funniest album about mental illness you will ever rock out to.

# SMARTEST BOOK
# BASEBALL TEAM VI
# The All-Presidential
# Baseball Team

### Owner: GEORGE W. BUSH (1946–)

Life imitates list and vice versa. George W. wasn't much on speechifying or even understanding or explaining policy. But he does love the old ball game. If he had been made commissioner instead of running for president, there would be a lot more living people living.

### Umpire: JIMMY CARTER (1924–)

When you win a Nobel Prize for Peace and get the Arabs and Jews to sign a peace treaty, you get to ump the game.

### Manager: FDR (1882–1945)

Franklin Roosevelt couldn't walk, but goddammit he could smoke—and try to restack the Supreme Court. A president who can get the Hoover Dam built can manage a ball team.

### Catcher: TEDDY ROOSEVELT (1858–1919)

Teddy "Speak softly and carry a big stick" Roosevelt can direct the pitchers and turn the ballpark into a wildlife refuge.

### First Base: RONALD REAGAN (1911–2004)

Ronnie was big, left-handed, and good-looking. All good for the first bag. Also, if we lose, he won't remember why—he'll just be full of team spirit. But he definitely can't be the union rep.

### Second Base: BARACK OBAMA (1961–)

Because he so easily slides to both the left and right.

### Third Base: BILL CLINTON (1946–)

Willy Clinton is a great baseball name. He can handle the hot corner. Plus, third is close to the stands, so he can troll for totty.

### Shortstop: ANDREW JACKSON (1767–1845)

Old Hickory was able to dig deep and move the Cherokee Nation. He can definitely dig for a grounder. Best hair ever for a president.

### Right Field: DICK CHENEY (1941–)

Dick was the rightest right winger ever to darken the White House. He covered up 9/11 and started an ill-advised war with Iraq. He can surely flag a pop fly.

### Center Field: JFK (1917–1963)

All the chicks can see you in center.

### Left Field: EDITH WILSON, Woodrow's wife (1872–1961)

Woodrow Wilson was so ill that Edith was de facto president for years. Our first Woman president gets to play left. You have to have a strong arm, baby.

# POETRY VIII
## Dante Alighieri
### (c. 1265–1320)

Dante fell in love with Beatrice at first sight when he saw her as a child; then again years later wafting down the streets of Florence. He lived in a tumultuous time when the pope was fighting the emperor, and he fought and took part in politics. He was exiled and married, but he never forgot Beatrice. "Beauty of Her Face" is about longing for her. Courtly love, what we might call chaste and unrequited love, was all the rage in the thirteenth century. Dante took time out from pining for Beatrice and fighting a losing war to write what is considered to be the most magnificent achievement in Italian literature. In *The Divine Comedy*, Dante is your personal guide through the circles of hell, heaven, and purgatory. Written in Italian rather than in Greek or Latin (as was the custom at that time), it is a breakthrough. As T. S. Eliot said, "Dante and Shakespeare divide the world between them; there is no third."

### Beauty of Her Face

For certain he hath seen all perfectness
Who among other ladies hath seen mine:
They that go with her humbly should combine
To thank their God for such peculiar grace.
So perfect is the beauty of her face
That it begets in no wise any sigh

Of envy, but draws round her a clear line
Of love, and blessed faith, and gentleness.
Merely the sight of her makes all things bow:
Not she herself alone is holier
Than all; but hers, through her, are raised above.
From all her acts such lovely graces flow
That truly one may never think of her
Without a passion of exceeding love.

# MOVIES IV
## The Comedies

Rarely honored with awards, comedy may be the most popular genre. We all want to laugh even if some people insist on laughing at puerile nonsense. Comedy can be profound and moving, but the main thing is to win the crowd.

### RUSHMORE
#### Wes Anderson, director, 1998

*Rushmore* is the best of director Wes Anderson's post-Salingeresque, '70s movie motif: vignettes, quirky lovable people, a decidedly fantasy take on school and young love and frustration and pain. A perfectly drawn little world we get to share and delight in. Max, played by Jason Schwartzman, is the most active student in his prep school, Rushmore. Not the best student, just the most enthusiastic. He writes plays based on '70s cop movies, is a member of every club, and is involved in everything. He meets a lovely teacher, Miss Cross, the captivating and grave Olivia Williams, who is recently widowed. Max fixates on her, just like he does everything else. He saves the Latin program because of a casual comment she makes, much to the disgust of the other students. He meets Herman, the tragically awesome Bill Murray, a lonely, wealthy man who has two sons he hates at the school. They bond until Miss Cross and Herman get together, and then it is revenge of the fifteen-year-old scorned. Bill Murray made the shift from comedy star to actor in this film. There is much to his hangdog expression and eyes full of pain. Where in earlier movies Bill Murray is the kooky life of the party, in *Rushmore* he gets tremendous response and plays not one thing for laughs. The profound triangle twixt him, Miss Cross, and Max is at the heart of this gem. Most comedies don't have the honesty to have adults treat the young like anything but annoyances or devices. *Rushmore* gives everyone equal emotional footing. The quirky, well-observed comedy has a zillion beautiful details like title cards to announce the passing of time and British Invasion music to capture the frothy feelings. Fanciful without a single tiger getting loose. This is a distinctly American comedy that will delight your heart.

## WITHNAIL & I
### Bruce Robinson, director, 1987

The Swinging '60s as seen through the eyes of two actors living in dire poverty in London. They decide to sponge off Withnail's crazy uncle Monty and spend a weekend in the country. They are utterly unprepared for what happens out there. Richard E. Grant is genius as Withnail, your worst best friend; he is vain, callous, wheedling, and hilarious. He is that friend who consumes all your drugs and then gets sick on the solvents under the sink. Paul McGann is *& I* (his name is never spoken), the victim of Withnail's whims and the unwilling recipient of Monty's lust because the ratty Withnail told his uncle he was gay. They cadge drinks, try to shoot fish, run from the locals, and create drama. Director and writer Bruce Robinson wrote this about his own life as a poor actor in London trying to survive a particularly lust-driven director and his mad roommate, Vivian MacKerell, a would-be star. If you drink along to this movie, be prepared to suffer calamitous consequences. Bonus: best drug dealer character in movie history played by Movie Helper Ralph Brown. What you have done is make your brain high—sit down, it will pass.

## THE THREE MUSKETEERS
### Richard Lester, director, 1973

There are a million versions of this movie, including one with Charlie Sheen as a musketeer. Dumas can be heard spinning in his grave. This '70s classic has the most humor and captures the period with a light hand. Richard Lester directed commercials, the Beatles' *A Hard Day's Night*, and *Help!* He wanted the Beatles in this, but it never happened, so instead he got Faye Dunaway as the lioness Milady de Winter, the dashing Christopher Lee as Rochefort, and those are just the sexy bad guys. The mad, bad, and dangerous Oliver Reed as the self-destructive brawler Athos and, yes, Raquel Welch—boom boom out go the lights. The dwarves at the court of the French king gossip under the plates they have stacked on their heads. Torturers get caught cooking potatoes in the fire where they heat their irons. A merry-go-round run by hand. The minutiae of the period is given full flow and add to the good times. Fun and thrilling, the movie will have you sword-fighting in the halls and wearing a giant floppy hat. It is actually two movies, *Three* and *The Four Musketeers*, that were shot at the same time; they split the movies in two without telling the cast. Everyone sued everyone. Nighttime sword fights, fights in a laundry, stolen chickens—it is true to Dumas but as zany as a Beatles movie. Irresistible. I know there are two Richard Lester movies. Write your own damn book.

## IGBY GOES DOWN
### Burr Steers, director, 2002

This is written and directed by Gore Vidal's nephew, Burr Steers (no real reason to mention that, it just seems like a cool thing to know). Kieran Culkin is hilarious as the put-upon Igby, who has been kicked out of every prep school on the East Coast. Ryan Phillippe brings it as the cold, stuffy yuppie brother who thinks he's useless. Susan Sarandon is divine as his wealthy checked-out mother who hates him, and look for Bill Pullman as his dad in a mental hospital. Igby is a super mess but also painfully honest and pretty bright. The world is too much for him. Astutely drawn, this is a picture about emotional unavailability and the crying need to connect. The obstacles are universal: wealth, drugs, jealousy, and the lies that every family keeps like heirlooms in a strongbox. Igby wants love, but his world is about achievement and success: two things he can't come to grips with. Jeff Goldblum, the king of Movie Helpers, plays D.H., his stepfather figure. Goldblum is an asshole banker who gets Igby a crib in New York. There Igby starts an affair with a confused girl, Claire Danes, and sleeps with D.H.'s junkie girlfriend, Amanda Peet. It gets even more complicated as the relationships change and ebb thick and fast. Drug deals, ODs, teen sex—this picture shines a more revealing light on the whole coming-of-age teen picture than a weekend at the Disney studios. Clever and morbid, utterly worthwhile.

## THE GENERAL
### Buster Keaton and Clyde Bruckman, directors, 1926

Buster Keaton was a prop in his parents' vaudeville act, ergo the name Buster. Keaton the director was a stunning technician as well as being wildly innovative. Mostly, he is dead funny. His sensibility plays modern because he never asks the audience to go it alone. Whatever mishaps befall him, he hits us with a silent plea, the look right to the camera. Sometimes that's the whole gag; sometimes it is the payoff. Charlie Chaplin is more sentimental, Harold Lloyd more middle class. Keaton sets himself up to be beaten and then shows us brilliantly how to come through. The effects he achieved and the unbelievable stunts he performed defy physics. He pours a train into a river, and he runs the length of a speeding locomotive. In this film his artistry as a writer, director, and performer is in full effect. Buster is an acrobat who flies and falls and never changes expression. He is beautiful, and his eyes say everything. As with Lon Cheney and Garbo and Gloria Swanson, the face carries the day.

You will laugh out loud at a sepia-colored movie. Keaton ain't sentimental, but he is arch in his own way. Start here and then watch a silent a month. You will come over to the quieter side.

# BASEBALL II
## What the Evil Old White Man Did

Organized baseball was started by corporate robber barons in the nineteenth century. That is why it is such an enduring American tradition. Baseball should ban white older men from owning teams. Here is a list of things the old white men who have always owned and operated Major League Baseball have been opposed to.

A) The radio. That's right, they presciently anticipated that if the games were broadcast for free, it would hurt attendance. Most teams had no regular radio presence till the 1940s. Even then, they didn't do all the away games but did cheap, in-studio re-creations. Our greatest senile president, Ronald Reagan, attained his firm grasp on reality in that atmosphere.

B) Letting anyone play who wasn't white.

C) Hiring proper paid umpires. In the nineteenth century, one ump worked the game. He was way behind the plate, so he didn't get clobbered with a foul ball. He more often got hit with bottles and food and drunkards running up to punch and beat him. Then when someone got on first, he moved behind the pitcher. Runners dashing from first to third rarely touched second, knowing the ump couldn't see everything. In other words, cheating ruled.

D) Paying the players as human beings. Players were chattel till just a short while ago. *Chattel* means "slave." The owners had a reserve clause allowing them to control who played for whom and for how much cake. It took till the 1970s and Marvin Miller, the labor negotiator, to organize the players into the strongest, most successful union in the United Snakes.

E) TV. Again, they felt suckers—meaning paying fans—wouldn't come and spend their hard-earned clams at the rotting stadiums that brooded over the wrecked cities then. You got one crappy game of the week in the '60s and '70s, and it was always the bloody Red Sox. We freely admit that football and basketball are way better TV shows.

F) Shouldering the blame for alcohol abuse, speed, steroids, and the fantastically acronamed PEDs, or performance-enhancing drugs. In the olden days players were often drunk on the field. So were the fans. Then came the newer days and amphetamine, so the players could play the mad six-month schedule. Then the '80s came and the players did lots of coke and the owners looked the other way and never offered substance abuse help. Then came 'roids. The players got huge and cranked giant homers. The owners watched, sat back, did nothing, and raked in the money for decades. Then the black man Barry Bonds broke the white guy Mark McGwire's single-season home-run record and the shit hit the fan. Then came the outrage: Barry Bonds invented cheating, he was the devil, he was arrogant to writers, he gazed lovingly at his soaring taters much as Rembrandt appraised his canvas after painting a masterpiece. So he had a Barcalounger and a TV in front of his locker—that didn't mean he was a demon. He was big, black, and didn't make it easy to get a quote. Notwithstanding the fact he was the biggest drawing card in baseball, Barry was pilloried. The owners blamed the players for doing what they wanted them to do. Get huge and make the game popular with people again. Hypocrisy is so easy and fun and easy.

G) Barry Bonds and Roger Clemens are the two best players of their generation. End of story. Did they use 'roids? Yes. Did everyone? Yes. Was it illegal when they did it? No. Are they any less moral than other players? Really? When you cheat at work by stealing a Post-it pad or eating someone else's lunch out of the fridge, it makes you an ass hat. When Barry and Roger cheated, small children cried tears of joy. You decide who is a bigger charlatan.

H) Playing baseball on the West Coast. The major leagues had no team west of Milwaukee for almost one hundred years. Guess they figured too many burning wagons and such.

I) Negotiating. There is a popular trope that goes, "I would love to be an athlete. I would play for nothing." Right. What happened to the love of the game and all? The truth is, everyone in every line of work negotiates to get the best pay they can all the time. The owners of all sports teams, who are mostly white and rich, with a very few exceptions, negotiate relentlessly to pay the concession workers less, to charge the fan more for tickets every season, to screw the towns they play in by threatening to leave unless the taxpayers buy them a new corporate revenue dome, and on and on. But if players, whose careers are limited, want to be compensated, they are greedy. That argument makes anyone sound like an angry, white, portly guy hosting a shouty all-sports radio show called *99 the Weasel* or *Petey and the Cracker.*

J) Anything good. Owners have turned ballyards into noisy, mindless, NASCAR-intelligence-level, nonstop-sensory-overload video game joints. Baseball is a stately, boring game with sudden breaks for action. Every moment doesn't have to be celebrated with giant ads and hideous music that sounds like a toaster dying. Parents and children can speak civilly to one another at a baseball game because only an organ is playing. Baseball at its best is church with spitting.

K) Children. Yes, that's right. The owners hate children. Kids don't understand what a lockout is. They cry when the team moves or a player is suspended or Tim McCarver is mixing a metaphor with a mistake. Tickets in L.A. are over $100 apiece to sit near the field down the line. Kids always have that kind of ready cash. Baseball is also notoriously racist and male. What is not for a young mind to love?

# POETRY IX
## William Blake
### (1757–1827)

Blake saw God when he was four. His parents were skeptical but did not make him go to school. So that worked. They taught him to read and write at home. Blake next saw a tree full of angels when he was nine. At ten, he announced he was going to be a painter, so the folks sent him to art school. He took up poetry and became an engraver's apprentice. One of his assignments was to sketch the tombstones at Westminster Abbey. He retained his Goth outlook as an artist his whole life. Blake was a real free thinker who detested governments and the church's tyranny. He wrote much about it and rolled with Thomas Paine, who helped start our revolution with his pamphlet *Common Sense*, and Mary Wollstonecraft, the noted feminist. Blake was working on illustrations for an edition of Dante's *Divine Comedy* up until his death. He remains a unique poet and talent. This joint is lengthy, but it rhymes and you have to bend some of the words to make them rhyme. I suggest the William Blake cocktail. Two ounces of anything hard. Wave your hand over the glass, gaze at the heavens, and swallow all at once. Then read this bear.

### Auguries of Innocence

To see a world in a grain of sand,
And a heaven in a wild flower,

Hold infinity in the palm of your hand,
And eternity in an hour.

A robin redbreast in a cage
Puts all heaven in a rage.
A dove-house fill'd with doves and pigeons
Shudders hell thro' all its regions.
A dog starv'd at his master's gate
Predicts the ruin of the state.
A horse misused upon the road
Calls to heaven for human blood.
Each outcry of the hunted hare
A fibre from the brain does tear.
A skylark wounded in the wing,
A cherubim does cease to sing.
The game-cock clipt and arm'd for fight
Does the rising sun affright.

Every wolf's and lion's howl
Raises from hell a human soul.
The wild deer, wand'ring here and there,
Keeps the human soul from care.
The lamb misus'd breeds public strife,
And yet forgives the butcher's knife.
The bat that flits at close of eve
Has left the brain that won't believe.
The owl that calls upon the night
Speaks the unbeliever's fright.
He who shall hurt the little wren
Shall never be belov'd by men.
He who the ox to wrath has mov'd
Shall never be by woman lov'd.
The wanton boy that kills the fly
Shall feel the spider's enmity.

He who torments the chafer's sprite
Weaves a bower in endless night.
The caterpillar on the leaf
Repeats to thee thy mother's grief.
Kill not the moth nor butterfly,
For the last judgment draweth nigh.
He who shall train the horse to war
Shall never pass the polar bar.
The beggar's dog and widow's cat,
Feed them and thou wilt grow fat.
The gnat that sings his summer's song
Poison gets from slander's tongue.
The poison of the snake and newt
Is the sweat of envy's foot.
The poison of the honeybee
Is the artist's jealousy.

The prince's robes and beggar's rags
Are toadstools on the miser's bags.
A truth that's told with bad intent
Beats all the lies you can invent.
It is right it should be so;
Man was made for joy and woe;
And when this we rightly know,
Thro' the world we safely go.
Joy and woe are woven fine,
A clothing for the soul divine.
Under every grief and pine
Runs a joy with silken twine.
The babe is more than swaddling bands;
Throughout all these human lands
Tools were made, and born were hands,
Every farmer understands.
Every tear from every eye

Becomes a babe in eternity;
This is caught by females bright,
And return'd to its own delight.
The bleat, the bark, bellow, and roar,
Are waves that beat on heaven's shore.
The babe that weeps the rod beneath
Writes revenge in realms of death.
The beggar's rags, fluttering in air,
Does to rags the heavens tear.
The soldier, arm'd with sword and gun,
Palsied strikes the summer's sun.
The poor man's farthing is worth more
Than all the gold on Afric's shore.
One mite wrung from the lab'rer's hands
Shall buy and sell the miser's lands;
Or, if protected from on high,
Does that whole nation sell and buy.
He who mocks the infant's faith
Shall be mock'd in age and death.
He who shall teach the child to doubt
The rotting grave shall ne'er get out.
He who respects the infant's faith
Triumphs over hell and death.
The child's toys and the old man's reasons
Are the fruits of the two seasons.
The questioner, who sits so sly,
Shall never know how to reply.
He who replies to words of doubt
Doth put the light of knowledge out.
The strongest poison ever known
Came from Caesar's laurel crown.
Nought can deform the human race
Like to the armour's iron brace.
When gold and gems adorn the plow,

To peaceful arts shall envy bow.
A riddle, or the cricket's cry,
Is to doubt a fit reply.
The emmet's inch and eagle's mile
Make lame philosophy to smile.
He who doubts from what he sees
Will ne'er believe, do what you please.
If the sun and moon should doubt,
They'd immediately go out.
To be in a passion you good may do,
But no good if a passion is in you.
The whore and gambler, by the state
Licensed, build that nation's fate.
The harlot's cry from street to street
Shall weave old England's winding-sheet.
The winner's shout, the loser's curse,
Dance before dead England's hearse.
Every night and every morn
Some to misery are born,
Every morn and every night
Some are born to sweet delight.
Some are born to sweet delight,
Some are born to endless night.
We are led to believe a lie
When we see not thro' the eye,
Which was born in a night to perish in a night,
When the soul slept in beams of light.
God appears, and God is light,
To those poor souls who dwell in night;
But does a human form display
To those who dwell in realms of day.

# MUSIC IV
## Folk

The communist movement and civil rights in America had a melody: the sincerity of Pete Seeger and the Weavers, the honest, unflinching humanism of Woody Guthrie. The Dust Bowl and the war had made the USA acutely aware that some had and some did not and never the twain. The folk music scene in New York is the consummation of black, rural, and ethnic sounds coming together in prison chants, union anthems, and folksongs with a message: freedom and equality are worth fighting for and singing about. Bob Dylan moved from the frozen wastes of Minnesota to the cauldron of New York City, where he played the joints and coffeehouses and reinvented himself from middle-class kid to troubadour and custodian of roots music. Folk music has a purpose, and it is the genuine pulse of rock, straight through to punk and rap.

### COURT AND SPARK
### Joni Mitchell, 1974

Joni Mitchell took no shit. A girl in a boys' world, she could write and smoke and roll with the dudes as well as anyone. Joan Baez is the conscience of folk, and Odetta the soul; Joni is a game of pool in the back room with some drugs and beer. She had a hit early writing "Both Sides Now" for Judy Collins and was set to launch. Quirky, poetic, jazzy, and idiosyncratic with her own unique delivery, timing, tuning, and bizarre sense of humor (yes,

Cheech and Chong, stoner comics emeritus, guest on this record). Joni Mitchell is in top form writing and singing and charming us. "Help Me" is amazingly sweet of her. "Free Man in Paris" is simply great pop. She went on to lay down the astounding *Hejira*, which is artier, but this album hits all the right notes melodic and dissonant. Get her and squeeze her and don't let her go.

## BLOOD ON THE TRACKS
### Bob Dylan, 1975

You have to have one Dylan album to prove you have heard of the twentieth century. From Woody Guthrie to Leadbelly, from Jesus to strip joints, Dylan is teaching a credit/no credit course on American music. His snide, nasal warble gets nastier with every hearing. Deep invective and hatred mingle with sweetness and even longing. All great artists find the humor in tragedy; Dylan puts the tragedy in  humor. Couples walk together in the park all the while being tangled up in blue. People disappear and reappear; there are too many words, it is all of a piece. The most challenging poet to sing pop music, Dylan is not on your wavelength: you are dared to tune in to his. You may need a drink to bolster yourself, and when the small man starts croaking about how all the people he once knew *are an illusion to me now*, you may need a tissue to catch the involuntary tears. Essential to your betterment.

# POETRY X
## Matsuo Bashō
### (1644–1694)

Bashō was a teacher and poet of seventeenth-century Japan. He favored seclusion and the countryside and, to understate the case, was a bit depressive. He, in essence, invented haiku, and his frog poem is the most famous of the tons he wrote. Bashō practiced Zen and is a definite influence on the Beat poets. In Japan, he is revered. His use of image is unsurpassed. The first poem is his most famous; the last poem is his farewell to us. In between, he explored the universe with rare economy and keen poetic intent.

> The quiet pond
> A frog leaps in,
> The sound of the water

.

> A cuckoo cries,
> and through a thicket of bamboo
> the late moon shines

.

> This bright harvest moon
> keeps me walking all night long
> around the little pond

the setting moon
the thing that remains
four corners of his desk

·

In the moonlight a worm
silently
drills through a chestnut

·

All my friends
viewing the moon—
an ugly bunch

·

falling sick on a journey
my dream goes wandering
over a field of dried grass

# SMARTEST BOOK
# BASEBALL TEAM VII
## The Women in History
## Baseball Team

**Manager: HARRIET TUBMAN (d. 1913)**

Tubman can give the steal-away sign like no other. She made nineteen forays to free slaves and rescued her own family. Sometimes she pulled a gun on reluctant fugitives, telling them, "You'll be free or die." That is decisive action. She is in charge.

**First Base: SACAGAWEA (d. 1812)**

Sacagawea was kidnapped as a child, and was the only Woman on the Lewis and Clark expedition. She interpreted, dug wild artichokes, saved their bacon more than once, and gave birth. She needs no help scooping grounders.

**Second Base: HYPATIA OF ALEXANDRIA (d. 415)**

Beloved scholar, teacher, and radical educator, Hypatia drove her own chariot and invented the astrolabe and the hydrometer. She ran afoul of Bishop Cyril by being independent and anaytical. Christian fanatics pulled her from her carriage and killed her. Cyril got made a saint; Hypatia got a better deal—a movie starring Rachel Weisz. We give her the beloved second sack to defend.

## Shortstop: MARIE CURIE (1867–1934)

Marie Curie won two Nobel Prizes. In different fields. Her husband, daughter, and both sons-in-law also won Nobel Prizes. She coined the term *radioactivity* and drove ambulances kitted out with X-ray machines to the front in WWI. She spent her prize money on helping the Allies. Her papers and effects remain dangerously radioactive. She glows like the universe, at short.

## Third Base: JOAN OF ARC (d. 1431)

Saint Joan was a teenage general and the savior of France. Inspired by spirits, she went to the king, took over the army, and had a spell of beating down the English. They say butterflies followed in her wake, and she wept over the wounded. Fierce and motivated by the highest principles, she is all-time at third.

## Left Field: SUSAN B. ANTHONY (1820–1906)

Susan B. was one of the great advocates for the equality of Women. Arrested, burned in effigy, and turned away by men—she would not be ignored. She traveled far and wide and petitioned the government ceaselessly for the right to vote. She spoke before every Congress from 1869 to 1906 to ask for passage of a suffrage amendment. She can organize left field.

### Center Field: LA MALINCHE (d. c. 1529)

Born to a noble family, La Malinche was captured and sold into slavery. She was given to Cortez during his run to Tenochtitlán. When he was told she spoke several languages, she was given the job as chief translator and negotiator. She gets a bad rap as a conspirator and traitor, but the Aztecs were imperious and the time was ripe for local tribes to rebel and join Cortez in trying to smash the empire. Doña Marina—as the Spanish called her—bore a son with Cortez and is, for good or ill, a mother of Mexico. She gets the call in the big field.

### Right Field: BETTY FORD (1918–2011)

A dancer and the smart one in the marriage with President Gerald Ford, Betty was an advocate for the Equal Rights Amendment and abortion. She was fiercely honest about her fights with breast cancer and addiction. She made it okay for people to be real about chemical dependency while maintaining a dignified stance. Forthright and brave, Betty Ford is the candid right fielder.

### Pitcher: HILLARY CLINTON (1947–)

Hillary has been a First Lady, the first First Lady to hold elected office, a senator, and a secretary of state. She is badassador eternal. She dominates the mound. She can bring it down the middle or skew either way if the going gets hot. Listed at 5'6"—no matter her height, she stands tall.

## Catcher: HARRIS "MOTHER" JONES (1837–1930)

Mother Jones lost her whole family to yellow fever. Then she moved back to Chicago, lost her shop and all her belongings to the Great Fire of 1871. She hit the road as a labor crusader and social activist. She was what we call "an agitator," meaning she fought for better working conditions for miners and to abolish child labor. She can catch all of it and give it back double.

The Women of History team has the least solid birthdates of any list. Do we really not value Women so much that we don't care when they were born? Maybe the ugly icky white men who keep history could have paid more attention. Oh, they couldn't. They were men, so they were thinking of themselves.

# BASEBALL III
## Satchel Paige
### (1906–1982)

> I'll be thirty-five this year, and I can only pitch
> as long as Satchel Paige. That gives me
> thirty-five more years.
> —Philadelphia Phillies pitcher Tug McGraw

Satchel Paige is an American hero, and one day, if you are good, he will be your hero as well. Paige is the most famous player from the Negro Leagues—leagues that existed because blacks and whites were not allowed to play together. Paige swung and swore. He struck guys out with crazy fastballs. He bragged and showboated and chased the ladies and made a bundle during the Depression when hardly anyone—much less a black man from the South—could do such a thing. He showed America that the black person could be everything the white was in that most narrow-minded and patriotic pastime: the old ball game. He had fun doing it. The greatest clown and showman and maybe the greatest pitcher ever. He persisted and endured countless shortings, slightings, threats, injustices, and nasty prejudice, and came through it all with humor and cool. He was not the first to break the color line in baseball, but he was the first to captivate hearts and minds by playing with, for, and against white folks for dozens of years while the evidence piled up that segregation was bound to fail in the end.

With Paige it is not just a matter of what he did, which is monumental—it is also a matter of what he might have done had he been allowed to play in the white leagues in his prime. He is the most colorful ambassador baseball ever produced, and he charmed the whole hemisphere with his wild individualism. That's why he is my hero. He had the bluster of Ali, the courage of Wilma Rudolph, the panache of Arthur Ashe, and the agelessness of Lena Horne. Like contemporaries Jesse Owens, the great Olympian, and Joe Louis, the champion boxer, he was a towering figure in sports, a Number 1 pitcher, as he would say.

Some people are described as "legendary," but Satchel Paige legendizes the word. He was the first black man to pitch in the American League, first to pitch in the World Series, first Negro League player in the Hall of Fame, and the writer of two autobiographies. He embodies longevity. One of his two bios he called *Maybe I'll Pitch Forever*, and appropriately so: he had a rubber arm that let him pitch for over forty years. Nolan Ryan, he of unflagging stamina and a million no-hitters, pitched a puny twenty-seven years. Paige's first game was in the 1920s and his last game was in 1965 (for real), and he was still packing them in. He kind of still is.

Leroy Paige had a rough start—he was born somewhere around 1906 to dire poverty in a shotgun house in Mobile, Alabama. He was the seventh of twelve children; his large family headed by his mother, the formidable Lula. Like Babe Ruth, he is a typical poor kid who climbs out of being barefoot and poor to make a huge name for himself. As a boy, he was a loner and a truant, and he hung around the river throwing rocks at everything, harder than anyone else. Like everything with him, where the nickname "Satchel" comes from isn't altogether certain. He started work as a child, carrying satchels on a stick at the train station, and so it may be there that the name was born. Eventually, he hit the streets and started hanging with an unsavory crowd. Caught stealing costume jewelry, he landed in children's jail, where he met a coach who turned him around and who realized his value as a star attraction. Under the guidance of Coach Byrd, Paige learned his wild style of high-kicking his giant right foot in front of him so he could whip the fastball in around it. Paige had found his calling as an ace pitcher. Tall and skinny and just a kid, in 1926 he got an offer from the Chattanooga Black Lookouts, and, with his mom's approval and the understanding he would send her money, he signed. Once he was in organized ball, he made the world take notice.

Paige's hallmark was brash cockiness and hilarious theatrics. He threw fast and with deadly accuracy. He could throw a ball over a bottle cap or gum wrapper with alarming consistency. Then tell you all about it. At the start of his career, he threw only fastballs, and he even painted the word *fastball* on the bottom of his shoe so the other team knew what was coming. His fastball had as many names as the Hindu gods: Thoughtful Stuff, the Bat Dodger, the Four-Day Rider, Peas at the Knees, and the Be-ball, because, as he said, "It be where I want it to be." His wild antics and sense of promotion were rocketing him to black ball stardom.

His marquee move was "Guaranteed to strike out the side." A sign would announce his eminence: "World's Greatest Pitcher Leroy Satchel Paige Guaranteed to Strike Out the First Nine Men or Your Money Back." Baby, this would sell the tickets. He would call in the outfield and sometimes had the infield sit down while he took care of business. Occasionally they played cards on the mound behind him. This outrageous showboating made the fans go crazy, and within a year his team was farming him out to pitch for other teams.

The notorious Gus Greenlee, a racketeer and numbers runner, one of a handful of blacks in '30s America with capital to run a ball club, signed him up. He built the first black-owned baseball park, and he started the second Negro National League. Greenlee was also the owner of the Pittsburgh Crawfords. The 1930s Craws are considered the greatest Negro League team of all time. Some call them the greatest *team* of all time.

---

### WILD TIMES AT THE CRAWFORD GRILL

Crawford Grill was Gus Greenlee's place, a hoppin' joint in the Hill district of Pittsburgh that all the jazz cats played, like Duke Ellington, Louis Armstrong, Ella Fitzgerald, and Sarah Vaughan. Superstar Lena Horne worked downstairs, and her father worked upstairs, where the numbers money was counted. "Numbers" is a catchall for an illegal lottery traditionally played by the poor, and Greenlee was in charge of that racket in Pittsburgh. You could bet as little as a penny on a series of three numbers taken from the totals of race-track betting printed in the paper. The counters had to deal with mountains of small change. The players ate and made the scene there after ball games. Just across the street in the barbershop, Paige would hold court all day, sending kids over to get food and beer so he could keep his stories going.

---

It was also here that Paige met his first wife, Janet Howard, working behind the counter. Greenlee paid for their wedding at the Grill. Bill "Bojangles" Robinson, the dancer, co-founder of the Black Yankees, and movie star partner to Shirley Temple, was the best man.

> If you want to know the truth, I wasn't the onliest one who could pitch in the Negro Leagues. I told them at Cooperstown we had a lot of Satchels, there were a lot of Joshes. We had top pitchers. We had quite a few men who could hit the ball like Babe and Josh. Wasn't any mebbe so.
>
> —Satchel Paige

The Crawfords ball club was loaded with Negro League stars: "Cool Papa" Bell, who was so fast he could turn the light out and be in bed before the room got dark, hit leadoff; affable Josh Gibson, the "Black Babe Ruth," was the catcher; tempestuous star Oscar Charleston, whom many consider to be one of the best players of all time, was finishing up his illustrious career and managing; and Paige was the ace and top draw on a team of big names.

Josh Gibson, described by Bill Veeck as "at the minimum, two Yogi Berras," and Satchel Paige are linked as teammates first as the greatest battery in black ball and later as rivals. They both went into the Hall of Fame, though Gibson was long gone by then. Josh was a good catcher and superb slugger and the easygoing lovable lug to Paige's showboat braggadocio. They played on the Craws and barnstormed in Central America, but Gibson came back to the States where he hit an alarming number of homers. He is said to have hit the ball all the way out of Yankee Stadium. He is the only man to do so. Paige faced Gibson in the Negro World Series of 1942. In his autobiography, he recalls walking a batter to load the bases and then Gibson coming up. Paige told him he would get only fastballs, and the first two pitches were blazing strikes. "One more to go, I knew Josh knew it. The crowd knew it. It was so tense you could feel everything jingling," Paige recalled. "The last one was a three-quarter sidearm curveball. He got back on his heels. He was looking for a fastball." It was knee-high on the outside corner. Strike three. "Josh threw that bat of his four thousand feet and stomped off the field." Gibson was always genial, but late in his career started to drink heavily and became broody and delusional. He died of a stroke or a brain tumor hallucinating he was going to be called up to the white big leagues. A very tragic end for the greatest Negro League hitter of all. Satchel and Josh were close buddies and friendly counterparts to the last.

Paige also barnstormed every year against Dizzy Dean. Dizzy was the bragginest, rowdiest, most popular player in white ball after Babe Ruth. The leader of the famous St. Louis "Gas House

Gang," Dean is the last pitcher to win thirty games in the National League. He also grew up poor in the South, picking cotton shoulder to shoulder with blacks, and he loved playing against Paige. They riffed, held mock arguments, imitated each other's exaggerated wind-ups, trash-talked each other, and pretended to fight with the umps. They put on a great show for the fans in L.A. and all over the country where there were no big league teams. Dizzy said of those days, "If Satch and I were pitching on the same team, we'd clinch the pennant by the Fourth of July and go fishing until World Series time."

> A bunch of the fellows gets in a barber session the other day, and they start to arguefy about the best pitcher they ever see. Some says Lefty Grove and Lefty Gomez and Walter Johnson and old Pete Alexander and Dazzy Vance. And they mention Lonnie Warneke and Van Mungo and Carl Hubbell, and Johnny Corriden tells us about Matty, and he sure must have been great, and some of the boys say Old Diz is the best they ever see. But I see all them fellows but Matty and Johnson, and I know who's the best pitcher I ever see, and it's old Satchel Paige, that big lanky colored boy. Say, Old Diz is pretty fast back in 1933 and 1934, and you know my fastball looks like a change of pace alongside that little pistol bullet old Satchel shoots up to the plate. . . . It's too bad those colored boys don't play in the big leagues, because they sure got some great ballplayers. Anyway, that skinny old Satchel Paige with those long arms is my idea of the pitcher with the greatest stuff I ever saw.
>
> —Dizzy Dean, 1938 interview

Sometime during the years of WWII, Dean got a triple off Paige in a charity game. Paige shouted at him, "I hope all your friends brought plenty to eat, because if they wait for you to score, they're gonna be here past dark. You ain't goin' no further." He retired the next three batters; like Dizzy once said, "It ain't braggin' if you can do it."

---

### PAIGE AND HIS WOMEN

All he's doing is living a sinful, shiftless life.
All I can do is keep writing and reminding him
to go to Mass and be careful of gambling
and the wild women out there.
—Lula Paige

Paige was the top draw in baseball. Chicks dug him. "I'm not married," he once said, "but I am in great demand." It had been a fun party at the beginning, but Satchel was—to put it mildly—not a mindful or attentive husband. He blew all the money he was making barnstorming. Paige spent a fortune on colorful suits, shotguns, fishing gear, big cars, and hunting dogs. In his heyday, he was making five grand a week, loads for the Depression, and he held on to little of the cash. He confessed, "I have trouble holding on to the old green." The marriage to Janet Howard was not a triumph; Paige catted around too much on the road. She finally served him divorce papers before a game at Wrigley Field in Chicago. Paige mistakenly signed it thinking it was a fan asking for his autograph.

He married another Woman, Lucy, in Puerto Rico and later divorced her, too. He met his third wife in a camera store in Kansas City, Lahoma Jean Brown. She had no idea who he was, and that got him going. This marriage was the one that lasted; he stayed married to her to the end of his life, and they had six children and a million pets and chickens.

---

Paige immediately got the idea that he could earn more money on his own than he could pitching for Negro League teams with their short, somewhat eclectic schedules. Paige split the Crawfords and became famous for "jumping" teams to join others that made better offers. Paige did a lot of this "jumping," or "barnstorming," over the span of his career. Paige played in a million places, threw literally thousands of games, and was the most famous black athlete, if not person, in the United States. Most importantly, he proved that he belonged everywhere he went.

He turned a job in the bushes of the segregated black sports world into an international platform, pitching from Mexico to Canada to Venezuela, and even made regular outings to North Dakota for a tournament where the owner gave him a car but then had to beg him to stop riding around with white girls in the daytime. So owners haven't changed. He lived with his wife Janet in a modified boxcar, since there was no black neighborhood. Paige claimed the Indians thereabouts took a liking to him and gave him snake oil with venom to rub on his arm, which he swore by his whole career.

The biggest semi-pro tourney in the 1930s was in Denver every year sponsored by the *Denver Post* newspaper. Satch brought lots of black players to the team there, and they dominated. He claims to have jumped to Venezuela in the '30s because he "didn't have a top-coat." While there, he was playing outfield and chased a ball into the tall grass, where he came face-to-face with what he thought was a boa constrictor (even though they live in trees), and the next time he encountered a snake, he picked up a stick and "beat the devil out of that snake," and because of this the runner scored. "The crowd chased me right out of the park and the manager of the club wouldn't pay me for the game." There's the truth and there is a great story; Paige never let one interfere with the other.

In 1937, Paige flew down to the Dominican Republic. (Paige's departure broke up the Crawfords and got Paige banned from the Negro Leagues, but he was never banned for long.) The Caribbean was even wilder than the Negro Leagues. The dictator Trujillo had some shady-assed hoods give Paige a suitcase containing thirty grand and told him to put together a team of black all-stars to play on the Los Dragones. To make it weirder, a voodoo priest from Haiti gave him a *wanga* to help him win (though later he found out it was an evil charm to make him lose). During the championship, Paige saw the armed soldiers on the field—not necessarily to protect the players. The militia fired rifles in the air during games and shouted, "El Presidente doesn't lose." On the day before the championship series, the team was locked in jail for the night so they wouldn't go out and party. They won the championship, but Paige's nervous stomach couldn't handle the strain of the lifestyle and the spicy food. He did note that black players were given respect in Latin America and allowed to eat and be with others, unlike in our beloved land of the free.

Paige threw hard, and for years all he used was a fastball with deadly accuracy. Then one day in Mexico, his arm went dead. He tried everything—hot baths, massage, rest, chiropractors—and then he finally shut himself in a room thinking it was all over at thirty-two. He was facing retirement and poverty while he was at the apex of his career. The Negro League teams he had spurned and jumped from were happy to see him beg a little. No job was forthcoming despite his huge popularity. "When you been at the top and hit the bottom, it's a mighty long fall."

His second act was just beginning. The Kansas City Monarchs' white owner, J. L. Wilkinson, whose partner was a Klansman (ironic, that), showed mercy and took him back. "I'd been dead. Now I was alive again," said Paige. They played him on the Monarchs B-Team, which immediately became known as the Satchel Paige All-Stars. He played first and couldn't hit, but fans came to the small towns to see him.

> I never threw an illegal pitch. The trouble is, once in a while
> I toss one that ain't never been seen by this generation.
> —Satchel Paige

Then one day he threw without pain. Hooray. He next learned a changeup for the first time in his career. Cool Papa Bell taught him the knuckleball, which Paige eventually came to throw even better than Bell. He rose from the ashes and became a star again, pitching in the Negro World Series in 1942 and 1946.

The Negro Leagues didn't bother with helmets, and they had a trifle more latitude in the kind of pitches one could hurl as compared to the majors. This was more than a little pine tar. You could straight out spit and do whatever you liked to the ball. Paige threw a fastball as hard as anybody, but when his arm went bad, he employed a bunch of trick pitches that he gave exotic names—the Hurryup Ball, Midnight Rider, Midnight Creeper, Two-hump Blooper, the aforecited Be-ball, Looper, Drooper, Nothing Ball, Jump Ball, Trouble Ball, the incredibly appointed Whipsy-dipsy-do—and he was just as effective. Players in the majors who faced him in the late '40s and '50s said he could still bring the hard one when he had to.

---

SATCHEL AND THE GREAT DiMAGGIO

I just got a hit off Satchel Paige,
now I know I can make it with the Yankees.
—Joe DiMaggio

Paige was pitching in a tourney in California when the young Joe DiMaggio from San Francisco got to face him. DiMaggio was the scourge of the minor leagues, crushing the ball and running up a sixty-one-game hitting streak on his way to the New York Yankees, a zillion World Series, Marilyn, and immortality. He got one fluke hit off Satchel. The Yankee scout wrote a telegram to the big club: "DiMaggio everything we'd hoped he'd be: Hit Satch one for four." Paige meant that much as a competitor.

The Negro Leagues were a triumph of personal courage and entrepreneurial spirit, but they are also a disgraceful chapter in American discrimination that lasted for far too long. Big league parks would rent to the Negro teams because they paid hard cash and they drew good crowds, especially when Satchel was pitching. The Washington Senators made $100,000 a year renting to Negro teams. They also didn't allow the black players to use the clubhouse.

> There's a couple of million dollars' worth of baseball talent on the loose, ready for the big leagues, yet unsigned by any major league. There are pitchers who would win twenty games a season, outfielders who could hit .350, infielders who could win recognition as stars, and there's at least one catcher who at this writing is probably superior to Bill Dickey—Josh Gibson. Only one thing is keeping them out of the big leagues—the pigmentation of their skin.
> —Shirley Povich, *Washington Post*, 1941

In the '40s, *Time* and *The Saturday Evening Post* ran articles about Paige, and those pieces—even with their racist stereotypes—reminded fans of how long he had been going and his greatness. And how funny he was.

> For the first time a white magazine had burned incense at the foot of a black man outside the prize ring. It changed Paige into a celebrity. He immediately developed into a matinee idol among Negroes in this country. *The Saturday Evening Post* made him ten times more famous than the black press had. He cashed in on it by becoming a one-man barnstormer. He brought people back to the ball game. He got blacks in the habit of going to ball games and spending their money. It

caught the eyes of Branch Rickey, who was a money
changer from way back.
— Ric Roberts, *Pittsburgh Courier*

WWII brought home the fact that minorities were being asked
to defend the USA without enjoying civil rights when they came
home. But that would soon change. Branch Rickey, the man who
ran the Brooklyn Dodgers, was scheming to do what no one had
done: bring blacks into the majors.

They said I was the greatest pitcher they ever saw . . .
I couldn't understand why they couldn't give me no justice.
— Satchel Paige

In the Negro Leagues, one of Paige's teammates was the young
Jackie Robinson. Jackie Robinson had a tryout with the White
Sox in 1942, and they thought he was worth fifty grand, but
they wouldn't pull the trigger. Eventually, though, he became
the first black man to play in the white big leagues. Jackie was
worried he wouldn't make the grade when he got signed in 1945.
He confided in Gene Benson, his roommate, who reminded him
of all the illegal pitches the Negro League allowed: "Jackie, just
remember one thing: where you're goin' ain't half as tough as
where you been."

For all Jackie's talent, Paige was the trailblazer, and he and his
compatriots of the first generation of black baseball stars were
the very face of the daring, jive-talking, crowd-pleasing style of
Negro League play that came to the big leagues and white fans.
The great paradox is that the success of the Negro Leagues led by
Satchel in drawing fans actually delayed integration, as the white
owners wanted that rental income.

Paige took Jackie's signing personally: "Signing Jackie like they
did still hurt me deep down. I'd been the guy who'd started all
that big talk about letting us in the big time. I'd been the one

who'd opened up the major league parks to colored teams. I'd been the one who the white boys wanted to go barnstorming against."

Despite his feelings, Paige said of Robinson, "He's the greatest colored player I've ever seen."

There were better players than Jackie: Monte Irvin was one. Josh Gibson thought he should be first. The truth is simply that Satchel Paige could not be the first black man in white baseball at that late date in his career, even if he was the best known. He was older and making more than almost any white player, and he would not have gone to the minor leagues for a year as Jackie did. Jackie had the temperament and character, and in the end he wanted that culturally important job. Jackie was a staunch visionary; Paige a veteran showman.

> When everybody's calling you ageless,
> you got time for those comebacks.
> —Satchel Paige

In 1948 at the age of fortysomething, he finally got the call from maverick owner Bill Veeck, and a year after Robinson made the Brooklyn Dodgers, Paige became a big leaguer.

Brought out to the park to audition for Veeck and manager-shortstop Lou Boudreau, Paige said he felt "numb." Boudreau asked him if he wanted to loosen up by running. Paige said yes, then remembered he hated running and ran a few yards, then came back. He threw for a few minutes and only missed the plate a couple of times. Boudreau, who won the AL MVP that year, stood in against him and couldn't do anything. Paige was signed for half a season and given a year's pay. He was finally in white baseball. Veeck told him, "I'm just sorry you didn't come up in your prime. You'd have been one of the greatest right-handers baseball has ever known if you had."

Paige pitched in relief for the Indians a few times, then was asked to start. He threw back-to-back shutouts, and they sold hundreds of thousands of tickets. He went on to a 6–1 record that season, and, most impressively, when the Associated Press writers voted for Rookie of the Year, Paige garnered several votes, which he was quite delighted by, but he said that he "wasn't sure what year the gentlemen had in mind." Some papers were horrible, calling it an affront to the game to have an old clown like him, some were exultant; one New York paper called him "a Paul Bunyan in Technicolor."

After Cleveland he played on the St. Louis Browns and got in the All-Star Game a couple of times. By now he was in his fifties, but he didn't stop. He caught on with the minor league Marlins in Florida again for Veeck. In 1965, at fifty-nine, hustler and owner of the Kansas City Athletics Charley Finley brought him back for one game. Paige was seated in a rocking chair in the bullpen and attended by a "nurse," but he still threw three big-league scoreless innings. They brought him out for the fourth, so he could take a bow. The crowd gave him a standing ovation as he walked off the mound. Paige always pleased the crowd. He is still out there inspiring us and making us love baseball.

---

### MONUMENTS AND WEEPING

The first professional Major League white team Paige played for, not a segregated team, was the Cleveland Indians of 1948. They also won the World Series. (The last time they did that little thing.)

Progressive Field in Cleveland has a monument park out back, and you may go there and stand in breathless wonder in front of his plaque or weep quietly as some sentimental *Smartest Book* types have done. For Satchel Paige put on a brave face in a bad situation and triumphed. With wit and humor.

Ted Williams, a baller who was nobody's sissy, had this to say when he was placed in the Hall of Fame: "The other day Willie Mays hit his five hundred and twenty-second home run. He has gone past me, and he's pushing, and I say to him, 'Go get 'em, Willie.' Baseball gives every American boy a chance to excel. Not just to be as good as someone else, but to be better. This is the nature of man and the name of the game. I hope that one day Satchel Paige and Josh Gibson will be voted into the Hall of Fame as symbols of the great Negro players who are not here only because they weren't given the chance."

Williams played on the Boston Red Sox for twenty-one years with breaks for two wars as a marine pilot. He is considered by many to be the greatest hitter of all time. He also played on a team that was the very last to integrate in 1959, a full twelve years after Jackie Robinson. Though the Boston Celtics basketball team was the first to field an all-black lineup and hire a black coach. The Sox owner Tom Yawkey just was not into it. In 1966, when Teddy Ballgame was elected to the Hall of Fame, it was only three years after the March for Jobs and Freedom on Washington where Martin Luther King gave his "I Have a Dream" speech, not that long after the march from Selma to Montgomery and the Watts riots. No white ballplayer had ever seized the day the way Ted did during his induction to the Hall. His speech lit a fire under baseball's collective ass, and within five years they started a special panel and put Paige and Gibson in the Hall.

When Paige was inducted, he got on the stand in his spectacles and his suit and said, "The only change is that baseball's turned Paige from a second-class citizen to a second-class immortal."

## PAIGE THE PHILOSOPHER

Father Time takes us all.
It took Satchel Paige and it'll take me.
—Bill "Spaceman" Lee

Paige was contemplative, and he philosophized on many topics. He even had a John Lennon–like quote about faith: "Don't pray when it rains if you don't pray when the sun shines." Then there is his dread of running: "I don't generally like running. I believe in training by rising gently up and down from the bench."

One of his more famous thoughts is, "How old would you be if you didn't know how old you are?" The question of age came up throughout Paige's career, and he would often reply, "I've said it once and I'll say it a hundred times: I'm forty-four." His mother, Lula, told a reporter that he was fifty-five rather than fifty-three, saying she knew this because she wrote it down in her Bible. Paige wrote, "Seems like Mom's Bible would know, but she ain't ever shown me the Bible. Anyway, she was in her nineties when she told the reporter that, and sometimes she tended to forget things."

Paige really quit the road only when he was in his sixties. As an actual old man he toured with the Indianapolis Clowns, who had featured Women players and a midget. He was the one wearing spectacles dispensing wisdom from the back of the bus and pitching an inning or two for disbelieving fans who thought he had passed. He then went back as a special coach to the Atlanta Braves, so he could get his pension.

Writer Richard Donovan printed a profile in *Collier's*

magazine called "The Fabulous Satchel Paige." This brought even more notoriety to our hero. It was 1953, and Paige had outlasted Ruth, Dizzy, and Bob "Rapid Robert" Feller. The best part of the rules is he followed so few of them.

Paige never said these things in this particular order, but when the legend becomes fact, print the legend. These are, in fact, on his family tombstone in Kansas City:

### How to Stay Young

1. Avoid fried meats that angry up the blood.
2. If your stomach disputes you, lie down and pacify it with cool thoughts.
3. Keep the juices flowing by jangling around gently as you move.
4. Go very light on the vices, such as carrying on in society. The social ramble ain't restful.
5. Avoid running at all times.
6. And don't look back—something might be gaining on you.

# SMARTEST BOOK
# BASEBALL TEAM VIII
## All-Time Negro League Team

᠎cᢁᢁ᠎

The Negro Leagues used lights to play at night way before the white leagues. They also had funner hangouts after the game. The teams were a source of pride for the black community, and on Sunday people put on their best clothes and went after church. It was a thing and a scene. Not a corporate revenue-flow situation.

### Manager: ANDREW "RUBE" FOSTER
### (1879–1930)

A great pitcher, Rube Foster helped establish the Negro League, taught Christy Mathewson the fadeaway, set the standard for coaching that white teams imitated. He became mentally ill but was absolutely monumental to black ball.

### Catcher: JOSH GIBSON (1911–1947)

The "black Babe Ruth" was lovable and could crush the pellet. If he had played in the white leagues, we would have an award named after him.

### First Base: WALTER FENNER "BUCK" LEONARD (1907–1997)

Big and bold, Buck Leonard batted cleanup behind Gibson and was deadly. They called him "the black Lou Gehrig" because he killed pitches.

### Second Base: FRANK GRANT (1865–1937)

The greatest nineteenth-century black player, Grant was classy and smooth around the bag. Played in the white minors for three years for Buffalo in 1886–88, but obviously never got called up.

### Third Base: WILLIAM JULIUS "JUDY" JOHNSON (1899–1989)

Judy Johnson was a star in the first Negro League World Series and a superb fielder. He was eventually voted into the white Hall of Fame. As a manager, he mentored Josh Gibson.

### Shortstop: JOHN HENRY "POP" LLOYD (1884–1964)

The papers called Pop Lloyd "the black Honus Wagner." Wagner said he was honored. No word on what Lloyd felt.

### Right Field: CRISTÓBAL TORRIENTE (1893–1938)

The Cuban Strongman could pitch, play second and third, and was the grooviest right fielder. Awesomely hit three home runs in a game against some barnstorming Yanks in Cuba. Babe Ruth was in right and demanded to pitch to Torriente after the second tater. Cristóbal promptly hit Ruth for a two-run double.

### Center Field: OSCAR McKINLEY CHARLESTON (1896–1954)

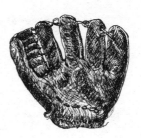

Charleston was maybe the best player in any league ever. He played center and could run, throw, hit for average, and cream the ball. They called him "the black Ty Cobb," but he was a much better fielder than Ty Cobb. Sam Lacy, the longtime writer for the *Baltimore Afro-American*, said he was better than Willie Mays. Hot.

### Backup Center Field: JAMES THOMAS "COOL PAPA" BELL (1903–1991)

I am not leaving Cool Papa Bell off this team. Not only does he have the best nickname in history but he was also the fastest cat to play ball. He batted lead-off, stole, and was so quick that he once stole two bases on one pitch. He played for more than twenty years and, even though at forty-three he was in a batting race, he sat out the last two games so the white scouts could get a look at Monte Irvin.

### Left Field: MONTE IRVIN (1919–)

Before Monte Irvin came to the white big leagues, he was the best left fielder for a decade in the Negro League. Missed three years serving in WWII—when he came back he hit .349, and the Newark Eagles won the pennant and beat Satchel Paige and the Monarchs in the Negro World Series. One of baseball's great gentlemen.

## PITCHERS

### LEROY "SATCHEL" PAIGE (1906–1982)

The king.

### RICHARD "CANNONBALL" REDDING (1890–1948)

"Cannonball" Dick Redding's hands were so huge he could hide a baseball in his palm. He threw hard, really hard. They brought him in to pitch to young Lou Gehrig to see if he could hit big league pitching.

### JOSEPH "SMOKEY JOE" WILLIAMS (1885–1951)

Smokey Joe Williams was half-black, half-Indian. He was in his forties when Satchel Paige saw him and declared, "That Joe could throw harder than anybody." Pitched a no-hitter at fifty-two. That is bad to the bone. His earlier nickname was "Cyclone Joe." You can figure out why.

### CHARLES WILBER "BULLET" ROGAN (1893–1967)

"Bullet" Joe Rogan didn't start pitching till age twenty-seven. He was a huge ace and also very fast. He led the league in steals at forty.

## RELIEVER

## HILTON LEE SMITH (1907–1983)

He had the fortune to be on the Monarchs with Paige and had the mixed fortune to be the man who came in and finished after Satchel threw the first three innings. A great pitcher, with or without Paige.

# MOVIES V
# The Sidney Lumet Corner

Martin Scorsese and Francis Ford Coppola are revered for their early work and quite rightly so, but Sidney Lumet stands with them in every way. He started as a child actor, and then a stage and TV director. His first film, *12 Angry Men*, is the story of a jury and the conclusions they jump to based on race and class. Lumet made it from TV to movies with that one and then made more than forty films outside the gates of Hollywood. Which made him distinct and kept his work singularly focused. A New Yorker, humanist, and moralist, Lumet captures a world filled with corrupt cops, crusading bank robbers, and people fighting a terrible system. These are the best of his best.

## DOG DAY AFTERNOON
### 1975

Al Pacino is Sonny, and John Cazale is Sal. They are robbing a bank in New York on a hot summer day. But it all goes mad from the start. The robbery becomes a media circus, a cause célèbre, and finally a cry for help. Sonny has a wife, kids, and a boyfriend who needs a sex change; that's why they are pulling the heist. The sweaty emotional honesty of the characters has you rooting for the crooks. Pacino towers in this role as a bisexual bank robber and Vietnam vet. Cazale's short Movie Helper career is written in the stars; he played in only a few movies (*The Godfather I* and *II*, *The Conversation*, *Dog Day Afternoon*, and *Deer Hunter*), but all were Best Picture material. This is one of the most powerful films of the '70s.

## NETWORK
## 1976

You're television incarnate, Diana,
indifferent to suffering, insensitive to joy. All of life
is reduced to the common rubble of banality.
—William Holden, *Network*

Shocking parody of TV that anticipates the dominance of reality shows and the commercialization of news as entertainment. Howard Beale (Peter Finch in his last role) is a raving-mad news anchor getting high ratings for his ranting. Diana (Faye Dunaway) is an insanely ambitious exec who convinces the boss to let her have Howard Beale and turn the news into a reality show with horoscopes, court TV, and Beale as a mad prophet. She also signs an active terrorist group to a reality show deal. Meanwhile, Max (William Holden) is Howard's boss and lifelong friend. He hates what's happening but still breaks up his marriage by having an affair with Diana. Sharp, pointed, caustic, and brilliantly acted. Peter Finch, Faye Dunaway, and Beatrice Straight (who plays Holden's wife) all copped statues. This picture calls out TV for what it is: a soulless vortex of greed and advertising. Stinging.

## SERPICO
### 1973

Every cop in New York is on the take except Frank Serpico (Al Pacino), and the rest of the NYPD would rather see him die than stand by while he blows the whistle on them. Gritty and uncompromising, Pacino is dogged in being the only good guy in a rotten world, subtle and sincere in the days when he specialized in that. This is also a true story of uncovering corruption and how the forces that be conspire and react with deadly force.

## THE VERDICT
### 1982

Lumet takes on the law and legality. Paul Newman shines as a drunk ambulance-chasing lawyer who gets tipped to an easy, open-and-shut medical malpractice case, but his conscience is awoken when he sees the victim in a coma and decides to do the right thing. Everyone is against him: the Catholic Church, the other legal team, even his girlfriend. A stirring courtroom drama that rages against the legal system and takes on life and death. Lumet hits a home run by casting Newman against his usual confident persona.

# THE SMARTEST DRUGS
# IN THE WORLD

> Reality is just a crutch for people
> who can't handle drugs.
> —Robin Williams

> I think that everything should be made available to
> everybody, and I mean LSD, cocaine, codeine, grass,
> opium, the works. Nothing on earth available to any
> man should be confiscated and made unlawful by
> other men in more seemingly powerful and advanta-
> geous positions.
>
> —Charles Bukowski

Drugs have a bad reputation. Drugs
mean people are dangerous and irre-
sponsible. This is puritanical nonsense.
Drugs have done everything from
cause Louis Armstrong to invent jazz to

make Maya Angelou outstrip you in every field of endeavor. Pres-
ident Obama said he regretted doing drugs, that they were bad.
Obviously, they messed up his life; he ended up with the menial
job of Leader of the Free World. President Clinton said he didn't
inhale and was impeached. W. Bush said he didn't remember if he
did cocaine; that is not something one forgets, because coke does
not just do itself. Elaborate measures are required. First, you have
to go to an asshole's house to get it. Even if you are a prince.

Everyone is on drugs. Your doctor, your friends, your doctor's friends, a certain author. Governments conduct wars on drugs. This is so they can waste tax money and shoot the poor with impunity. Many jobs have drug testing. No heads of corporations have to take a drug test. This is so people will feel awful about themselves and their awful bloody jobs and want to take drugs. Drugs don't make the users illogical. They make the people who want to monitor the users illogical. Remember: only users lose drugs, so make sure you have a safe place where you won't forget.

Maybe drugs just need a new name. We'll call them cat snacks instead. Are you holding any kitty snickers? How much for a dime bag of cat snackies? You know what would make that Daft Punk show even better or even good? A couple of snacks *de chat*. Here are some of *The Smartest Book*'s favorite kitten friskies:

## Weed

Being high is fun. TV is watchable sorta. Books are fascinating. Butterflies whisper messages if you smoke enough. There is being high and not being high. You have been not high. Try being high. Don't use if it makes you paranoid. But then just remember: it's you, not them. Well, I guess it could be them.

## Hash

Weed's exotic cousin. Make sure you have a colorful hat and a rug to nap on. Order the dates with bacon. Stop using if you start chanting.

### Cocaine

Use only if you have an evening to ruin. You will not meet the right kind of people. If you think they are the right kind of people, then coke has fooled you.

### Heroin

Oxymoronic paired with "chic." Only fun in fiction. No one who has ever done it recommends it as a party starter. Have a drink instead and read about it.

### Meth

Use only for short bursts of mania. Desist if you feel the inclination to shoot a road sign.

### Xanax

Use when directed to. Makes flying less stressful. Makes work groovy. With wine makes Bravo genius.

### Codeine

Use only until you run out. Don't call me crying.

### Molly

We think it is the same as Ecstasy. Maybe it's our age.

### Ecstasy

Ecstasy is better as a state than a drug. Hydrate often.

### LSD

Best in a safe place like the beach at night. Or under a blanket fort. Listen to Bebel Gilberto bossa nova jams. This will calm you.

### Mushrooms

Go to a park. Bring a kite. Meet the lower-flying deities on their own terms. Hydrate with magic tea.

### Miao Miao

We are too old to consider snorfing this. Do not ingest anything you can buy on a Dutch website.

### Laudanum

You are a nineteenth-century author. Write an epic poem with "Xanadu" in it.

# SMARTEST BOOK
# BASEBALL TEAM IX
## Dictators Baseball Team

Dictators have it tough. They have to be strong but are misunderstood by the innocent people they slaughter and oppress. Paradoxically, they hold together some nations with an iron will and law and order, but when those nations are set to take leave of them, all hell breaks loose like Marshal Tito in the Balkans or Saddam Hussein in Iraq. It is difficult not to make sport of them as they are like a morbid funhouse version of our so-called leaders. If Dick Cheney wore a funny hat and a leopard dashiki, we might all be laughing instead of looking over our shoulders. Let's round up these scoundrels and make a pennant contender out of them. Raise the flag, hide your dissidents, and let's play ball.

### Manager: ADOLF HITLER (1889–1945)

The most overused figure in history. The left use him to represent madness, genocide, and fascism; the right, to represent anything they disagree with. He was a sad, mediocre, freaky sadist, lousy artist, pedestrian soldier, maniacal, one-gonad, flatulent vegetarian who abused his niece so much she took her own life. He loved his dog and hated his spongy nephew Willy who, for real, came to New York and tried to break into society on his uncle's hot name. Dolf managed because Germany got organized fast and in short time did what Napoleon tried to do (beat up Europe), but then he made the same mistake of taking on Russia in winter. Hitler will have his coaches whip this team into shape. When he gets angry, he will toss the vegetarian buffet over. Then try to beat the Reds.

## Catcher: MANUEL NORIEGA (1934–)

One of the great Reagan/Bush era drugs-for-guns-and-money dictators. He ruled Panama and rigged every election; this cat can call a game. He was hounded out of his compound by U.S. forces blaring loud rock music, including Van Halen. He can definitely deal with the racket of a Fourth of July doubleheader. No need to drug test; he is super positive. The first foreign leader to be convicted in a U.S. court, this is a catcher who will get the most out of instant replay. No small nugget will get by him.

## First Base: RAFAEL TRUJILLO (1891–1961)

Part of that legendary all-star team of Latin American dictators with Pinilla from Colombia and the Somozas in Nicaragua, Trujillo ruled the Dominican Republic with brutal efficiency. Slaughtered loads of people, including the Haitians, who lived next door. He also hired Satchel Paige and a group of black stars to play for him in the '30s. He loved the game almost as much as stealing and cruising in his blue Chevy Bel Air. Alas, it was in the Bel Air that he was assassinated. Trujillo will keep runners close to the bag. With ruthless force if necessary.

## Second Base: NAPOLEON BONAPARTE (1769–1821)

Napoleon wasn't as short as rumored, more like close to 5'7", but he was as ambitious. As a young officer, he took initiative and ran with it. He was impatient at his own coronation and grabbed the crown before the pope could place it on his head and made himself emperor. Hits up the middle are nothing to him. He withstood Prussian guns, so he can take a hard slide and turn the pivot. You can bench him; he is used to exile. He may just come charging back out of the dugout and take over the world in between innings.

## Third Base: SUHARTO (1921–2008)

The dictator of Indonesia for thirty-two years. Because his reign coincided with the Vietnam War and he was not a commie, we gave him billions of dollars, all of which he absconded with. He gradually took over for Sukarno when a coup failed, so he has the soft hands needed for third. As far as gobbling up grounders, when he died it is said that he had embezzled somewhere between 15 and 35 billion clams, so he can suck it up hard. Toward the end after he stepped down, he said he was ill, but everyone saw him golfing and jogging so he is game-fit. A thief to catch line drives down the left-leaning line.

## Shortstop: FERDINAND MARCOS (1917–1989)

Shifty and self-serving, he is perfect to run into the hole for a grab. He perfected stealing, and his wife, Imelda, can be the equipment manager. She famously owned several skyscrapers and thousands of pairs of shoes. Marcos claimed to have fought the Japanese as a guerrilla during WWII, but guess what? He lied; he was, after all, a full-on lawyer. His wicked ways mean hot defense.

### Left Field: VLADIMIR LENIN (1870–1924)

The Lefty's lefty. Born to play the wall and fervent in his belief. Demanded absolute silence while he worked, so let's make some noise and inspire him to madness out there in the green acres. The man who gave us the Red Terror, purges, and the execution of the Romanovs can cut runners down at the plate with his strong arm.

### Center Field: AUGUSTO PINOCHET (1915–2006)

Pinochet seized power from the legally elected president Salvador Allende and had him aced. The general will not be shy in the vast reaches of center. Backed by the U.S., he willingly takes support and is a team player. Do not argue with him, or you will find yourself disappeared. Looks great in a uniform. He gets the call. If it is a blooper, he will *junta* it down.

### Right Field: IDI AMIN (1925–2003)

His Excellency President for Life, Field Marshal Al Hadji Doctor Idi Amin, VC, DSO, MC, Lord of All the Beasts of the Earth and Fishes of the Sea, and Conqueror of the British Empire in Africa in General and Uganda in Particular can now add right fielder. He was a notorious butcher and strongman. He rose through the ranks of the British Colonial Empire Army and snuck into power while the leader Obote was abroad. He has the wiles to play the far reaches of the park with all its quirks. Spent his last days with our staunch allies the Saudis so he could relax in the sun. The lord of the beasts will now be lord of the flies.

### Pitcher: FIDEL CASTRO (1926–)

Castro, strangely a righty, was known to throw a hard curve. If we had let him play, all this might never have happened. Legend is he tried out with the Yankees or Senators. He mythically turned down a $5,000 bonus to sign with the Giants—ten years later: pow, bang, ouch. Of course, he should have pitched for the Reds. Then the revolution may have gone down quite differently. Cuba regularly drubs international squads while maintaining Castro's horrible policy that forces Cuban players to defect. Castro once suggested that Jeb Bush, President George W's brother, could lose some weight, so leadership is not an issue. He is the obvious starter as the most famous baseball-playing aficionado dictator of all time.

### Relief Pitcher: JOSEF STALIN (1878–1953)

He is the ultimate stopper. Of humanity.

### Designated Hitter: CHAIRMAN MAO (1893–1976)

He took the Long March, he slammed his people with the Cultural Revolution, he chased girls on the road. He was built to smoke in the clubhouse and then get out there and take his cuts. He wrote the Little Red Rulebook.

# POETRY XI
## Inuit Poetry
### (Seventeenth Century)

The Inuit (Eskimos, as we have called them), were a nomadic hunter society that developed an oral tradition of singing to explore the vagaries of life and nature. Zealous missionaries put their bloody paws all over it, but certain elements survive to this day. We, the moderns and the citified, are not the only ones to feel the futility of our time here.

### Inuit Song

The great sea has set me in motion.
Set me adrift,
And I move as a weed in the river.
The arch of sky
And mightiness of storms
Encompasses me,
And I am left
Trembling with joy

## Song by a Woman

Long will be my journey
on the earth.
It seems as if
I'll never get beyond
the footprints that I make . . .

# MUSIC V
## Country & Western

This is white people's blues. Our understanding is that every single country artist has been visited by the same world of hurt. Their truck simply will not start, and it is not at all certain their dog is going to survive either, and their Woman has done left them. As a result of these horrible, hideous, unforeseeable circumstances that fate has dealt them, they gots to go to the honky-tonk all night long. No golden ray of sunshine beams down upon this world. Theirs is an unceasing veil of tears. Jolly for us their own respite is to give voice to their troubles in song.

### MODERN SOUNDS IN
### COUNTRY AND WESTERN MUSIC
### Ray Charles, 1962

> Music is about the only thing left that people
> don't fight over.
> —Ray Charles

It isn't enough that Ray Charles was born to abject poverty, lost his sight as a boy, lost his brother to drowning, and lost his mother when he was just fifteen. A horrific childhood, but he survived it with music. A prodigy who became mentored by a teenage Quincy Jones, Charles was hailed as a musical genius by thirty. He basically invented soul music but also became wildly influential in jazz, blues, R&B, rock, and gospel. He sold a jillion records

261

and won awards in every decade, but he also had twelve children with nine different Women, got busted for heroin, and struggled with the drug for years. Most awesomely, the state of Georgia made a version of his "Georgia on My Mind" the official state song. But that just gets us to this story's opening, as on top of all that, he reinvented country music and made it popular again in the early '60s by making the swinging and heartfelt *Modern Sounds in Country and Western Music*. A black man reinvigorated country music. By the way, he followed it up with Part Two a little later. He had the people at his label send him hundreds of country songs so he wouldn't pick only ones he was familiar with. He listened to hours of music and then settled on these tracks. His soulful rendition of Don Gibson's "I Can't Stop Lovin' You" made country music a factor again. He wails it like gospel blues with lush strings, lavish background vocals, and then invites them to "sing the song, children." Willie Nelson said this album did more for country music than any one album has ever done. He took white people music and made it everybody people music. This is before blacks and whites could eat at the same restaurant together in many places in the USA. It is a statement, his homage to the South he grew up in, and a declaration that no song escapes his magnificent rendering. Ray Charles took Hank Williams and put a big band on it. A true giant making a giant record. Get it and open a beer. Have a handkerchief ready for the tears of joy. Then go out and obtain *Modern Sounds in Country and Western Music 2*.

## LIVE AT FOLSOM PRISON
### Johnny Cash, 1968

I love songs about horses, railroads, land, Judgment Day, family, hard times, whiskey, courtship, marriage, adultery, separation, murder, war, prison, rambling, damnation, home, salvation, death, pride, humor, piety, rebellion, patriotism, larceny, determination, tragedy, rowdiness, heartbreak and love. And Mother. And God.

—Johnny Cash

He wore black because other singers wore rhinestones. He took massive drugs and fought with record executives. He looked like hell from too much speed and smokes. He was trying to clean up. He had a novel idea. He had played prisons all through his career—why not make a live record in one? Bob Johnston at Columbia Records made the call. Folsom Prison answered first. Johnny Cash had a huge hit early in his career with "Folsom Prison Blues" that has the immortal line of darkness and despair that any gangster poet would be proud to have written: "I shot a man in Reno, just to watch him die/When I hear that whistle blowin', I hang my head and cry." The date was set and two shows planned. He brought his not-yet-wife and partner, June, and the whole Johnny Cash stage show, including rockabilly luminaries Carl Perkins and his brother Luther Perkins. June tamed the cons and read a poem. Think about making a record in a prison in the '60s. People made live recordings at concert halls and nightclubs for nice people or at least unincarcerated people. Johnny Cash is a key voice for the underclass in American music. Murder and mayhem on the mainstream radio. The real world exposed in a train track shuffle. Guys take coke and shoot their girlfriends, men watch their own gallows being built, and then he sings a comedy song about a dog he hates, "Dirty Old Egg-Suckin' Dog." You hear cons being hailed on the PA system. He coughs, he clears his throat, he whoops and shouts off-key. The band finishes songs at various times. The crowd of prisoners is ecstatic—someone cares enough to come and sing about them. In an astounding moment, he sings "Greystone Chapel," a song by Glen Sherley, a lifetime criminal and one of the cons in the audience. He did not know that Cash had been given the song by the prison chaplain and had learned it the night before. In a tragic postscript, Sherley was helped by Cash and let out of prison and joined the band, but was too damaged to play well with others. The stint with Cash was short; he ended up taking his own life years later. This album is a thrilling document of an outrageous gig.

# POETRY XII
# Emily Dickinson
### (1830–1886)

Today, Emily Dickinson is acknowl-
edged and venerated, but in her lifetime
she published only a handful of poems.
Reclusive at best, in later life she spoke
to people through doors. Nonetheless,
she is a prolific poet and on her passing
left forty notebooks with thousands of

poems. An enthusiastic gardener and botanist, she kept a garden of
exotic flowers at her family home in Amherst. She often included
flowers with her verse in her correspondence. In death she has
found the renown she could not have hoped to ask for in life. We
are all for hope, and Miss Dickinson clung to it with something
close to fervency. She is our light in the hour of darkness.

### "Hope" is the thing with feathers

"Hope" is the thing with feathers—
That perches in the soul—
And sings the tune without the words—
And never stops—at all—

And sweetest—in the Gale—is heard—
And sore must be the storm—

That could abash the little Bird
That kept so many warm—

I've heard it in the chillest land—
And on the strangest Sea—
Yet, never, in Extremity,
It asked a crumb—of Me.

# MUSIC VI
# Rock and Reggae

Rock has always been around the edges of country and rhythm & blues. Mix in some vaudeville and sex and pow, it's a hit. The music the kids had been waiting for.

Reggae started up in Jamaica, landed in England, and had gone through many incarnations such as rocksteady and ska long before we heard it stateside. Then Bob Marley became the poster child but with an agenda and poetry, and we couldn't get enough.

### THE BAND
### The Band, 1969

They were a teenage bar band in Canada called the Hawks. The leader was a transplanted American rocker named Ronnie Hawkins who promised the boys "no money but more pussy than Sinatra." They played all night and rehearsed the rest of the night. The Hawk was strict, and they couldn't bring girlfriends to gigs as it would cut down on the willing chicks in the crowd. They could drink and pill, but he hated pot, afraid they would get done by the Mounties. Eventually, they split him and formed their own group. Dylan caught them and took them on tour. It was Dylan's after-folk electric tour, and they got booed every night by devoted folkies. Levon Helm, the drummer, split and worked on an oil rig. But he finally succumbed and came back to play and make the record. They rented a house in upstate New York and made a sprawling album with Dylan called *Music from Big Pink*. The

Band had a unique attack with three lead singers, Levon, Richard Manuel, and Rick Danko. The organist, Garth Hudson, was an accomplished musician and had to be paid ten bucks extra a week when he joined so his family wouldn't be disappointed by him joining a rock band. Together they had a studied, shambly sound with little of the then-current psychedelic information most bands were doing. They played all sorts of instruments when recording, switching off for unusual sounds. A bit rustic, countryish, and definitely historical, they wailed a ballad about the Civil War called "The Night They Drove Old Dixie Down" and had "King Harvest" about unionizing sharecroppers in the 1920s. This was not your typical rock band. George Harrison loved them, and Eric Clapton wanted to join them. They are white soul. Go there and find a cabin to dwell in.

## ARE YOU EXPERIENCED?
### The Jimi Hendrix Experience, 1967

He had put time in with the Isley Brothers band and the U.S. Air Force. He left for England and evidently they knew what they had. Jimi Hendrix is the shaman of psychedelic rock and a virtuoso who made all the English guys ashamed to be guitar heroes. A left-hander who played a right-hand guitar upside down for starters and the peacock of groovy gear, Hendrix played better, more inventively, and was better looking than anyone. This album asks many questions, and they almost all have to do with drugs. Hendrix's sound is still a tidal wave of feedback, squalling, and rhythm & blues. Paul McCartney recommended him for Monterey Pop, where D. A. Pennebaker was making a documentary, and Jimi lit the place up. "Purple Haze," "Foxey Lady," "Hey Joe," and "The Wind Cries Mary" do a lot of the lifting. Hendrix is so seductive and majestic as a singer, it is hard to believe he was shy about his singing in the studio. Apparently there were girls everywhere he went, what a surprise. Jimi Hendrix may be the greatest rock star and this album is why. One measure of a new sound is whether it still seems sonic after grunge, techno, postpunk, etc. This album is still, as they would have said then, "Heavy."

## THE HARDER THEY COME
### Various Artists, 1972

Reggae has its own constitution written on wax. *The Harder They Come* is the soundtrack to the movie of the same name. A low-budget but realistic picture about pot, bicycles, music rip-offs, and how rough the ghettoes of Kingston are. No one had seen poor people shoot at each other riding Vespas at the movies before. It was a sensation. Jimmy Cliff is the star, but the record is a compilation of late '60s and early '70s seminal reggae singles such as "Pressure Drop" by Toots and the Maytals and "Israelites" by Desmond Dekker & the Aces. This record made reggae go worldwide. Jamaica had been churning out this music for ages, but it took this record to go global. This album was de rigueur for all hipsters to have on their shelves in the '70s. Bob Marley may end up being the most amazing star reggae produced, but this album has it all. Thrills, chills, and run-ins with the cops. Jimmy Cliff has a beautiful, soaring voice and a lovely message of positive thinking, but the final word has got to go to Desmond Dekker: "I don't want to end up like Bonnie and Clyde." Warning: this album may require that you spark a massive spliff for max enjoyment.

# POETRY XIII
## Carl Sandburg
### (1878–1967)

Born to Swedish parents, young Carl started hauling milk at thirteen. He was a bricklayer, farmhand, soldier, journalist, biographer, historian, collector of folklore, socialist, civil rights activist, keeper of Lincoln, and undeniable, irreplaceable American. He was a journalist in Chicago, and once upon a time in America, we were all taught this poem. In these less literate times, we all don't learn it now. So here goes:

### Chicago

Hog Butcher for the World,
Tool Maker, Stacker of Wheat,
Player with Railroads and the Nation's Freight Handler;
Stormy, husky, brawling,
City of the Big Shoulders:

They tell me you are wicked and I believe them, for I have
    seen your painted women under the gas lamps luring the
    farm boys.
And they tell me you are crooked and I answer: Yes, it is
    true I have seen the gunman kill and go free to kill
    again.
And they tell me you are brutal and my reply is: On the
    faces of women and children I have seen the marks of

wanton hunger.

And having answered so I turn once more to those who
sneer at this my city, and I give them back the sneer and
say to them:

Come and show me another city with lifted head singing so
proud to be alive and coarse and strong and cunning.

Flinging magnetic curses amid the toil of piling job on job,
here is a tall bold slugger set vivid against the little soft
cities;

Fierce as a dog with tongue lapping for action, cunning as a
savage pitted against the wilderness,

Bareheaded,
Shoveling,
Wrecking,
Planning,
Building, breaking, rebuilding,

Under the smoke, dust all over his mouth, laughing with
white teeth,

Under the terrible burden of destiny laughing as a young
man laughs,

Laughing even as an ignorant fighter laughs who has never
lost a battle,

Bragging and laughing that under his wrist is the pulse, and
under his ribs the heart of the people,

Laughing!

Laughing the stormy, husky, brawling laughter of Youth,
half-naked, sweating, proud to be Hog Butcher, Tool
Maker, Stacker of Wheat, Player with Railroads and
Freight Handler to the Nation.

# MUSIC VII
## Jazz

❦

You need to get hip to jazz. If it seems dissonant and complex, it surely can be. It also swings and is lilting and romantic. Do not be afraid of jazz, little one. Dive right in. Jazz requires your attention for several reasons: it is the only indigenous American art form combining brass band, blues, slave shouts, and Caribbean music with classical European instruments like saxophone and bass. This music was born in bars and houses of ill repute. Pour a drink and light a smoke and spin some wax, cat.

### BIRTH OF THE COOL
### Miles Davis, 1957

Jazz morphed into swing when white radio got ahold of it, and then the big bands were born. Benny Goodman, the Dorsey Brothers, Duke Ellington, and a million others. Bands were huge with dozens of players and even a few girl singers. After the second ugly war, big band had to give way to bop as it was blacker and faster with Charlie Parker blowing more notes than anyone. In 1948, a bunch of cool cats met at the great jazz pianist Gil Evans's tiny crib behind a Chinese laundry. These meetings led to the Miles Davis Nonet, or nine. Miles had spent time in Charlie Parker's band after Dizzy split. They decided to harmonize, slow down the tempo, and generally shift big-band arrangements to a more arty form. They got a gig opening for Count Basie at the Royal Roost, and that's where Capitol Records heard them and offered them a chance to put it all on wax. Basie had dug the nine, though he thought it was more classical than jazz. They made the record on what was called 78 rpm and all the songs are about three minutes long. Gil Evans and Miles would make more records, but this one starts a whole movement called cool jazz. It is called this because it is cool. It sounds sad and feels cool. The musicians wear dark suits and take their craft very seriously while letting the music snake out like magic. You must attempt to be cool. Put on shades, pour a drink, light something even if it is a candle, and see if this record does not delight you. *Birth of the Cool* was recorded in 1949 and 1950, but the squares at the label sat on it till Miles was worldwide. By 1957, we had rock 'n' roll and *On the Road*. The time was right. The riff was ripe.

## THE COMPLETE ELLA FITZGERALD SONG BOOKS
### Ella Fitzgerald, 1956–1964

I never knew how good our songs were
until I heard Ella Fitzgerald sing them.
—Ira Gershwin

Jazz and Ella are the swingin'est four-letter words you need to know. All the great American composers get made better over the course of these eight magisterial albums. Pop music in the Jazz Age was the music of George and Ira Gershwin and Jerome Kern and all; the people who wrote musicals for the stage and screen were the pop hit songwriters of the day. These albums were arranged and packaged to showcase the songwriters' work by one of the great vocalists of all time. It is a perfect meeting of top-notch material, great arrangements, and the ultimate interpreter. Norman Granz was the owner of the legendary Verve label and Ella's manager. He was a visionary in terms of how his black acts were treated: he allowed no gigs in segregated places and demanded equal treatment in hotels and restaurants. He also had the creativity and wherewithal to get the best arrangers for this epic set. Duke Ellington and Billy Strayhorn arranged all the songs for their *Songbook*. It spanned eight years, but Ella conquered this mountain of American Standards, and now you have something exquisite to spin while you light candles for that dinner with someone special.

---

THIS IS ELLA ON MARILYN MONROE.
SOMETHING COOL YOU DIDN'T KNOW.

"I owe Marilyn Monroe a real debt," Ella later said. "It was because of her that I played the Mocambo, a very popular nightclub in the '50s. She personally called the owner of the Mocambo and told him she wanted me booked immediately, and if he would do it, she would take a front table every night. She told him—and it was true, due to Marilyn's superstar status—that the press would go wild. The owner said yes, and Marilyn was there, front table, every night. The press went overboard. After that, I never had to play a small jazz club again. She was an unusual woman—a little ahead of her times. And she didn't know it."

---

## WINTER IN AMERICA
### Gil Scott-Heron, 1974

No one can do everything,
but everyone can do something.
—Gil Scott-Heron

He is called the "godfather of rap music" for his driving poetry and social content. He has been sampled a zillion times by rappers. But they don't always have his power. Gil Scott-Heron wrote "The Revolution Will Not Be Televised." The message was humorous and radical and to the moment. Gil Scott-Heron's father was a professional footballer, the first black man to play for Celtic in Glasgow. Gil grew up being raised by his mother in Tennessee and later in New York. While attending university, he took time off to write two novels, *The Vulture* and *The Nigger Factory*. This is before he became the musician and educator of America for a generation; he can safely be called an overachiever. His poetry is revealing and always honest, his voice deep and delightful. His collaborator on many of his records was Brian Jackson, whom he met in college. This album has "The Bottle," an infectious beat, and is a devastating indictment of the destructive power of drink, a Woman's right to choose, and prison. It was also a catchy hit, and he described it in his usual frank way, "Pop music doesn't necessarily have to be shit." No, it does not, and everyone from Public Enemy to Kanye West has taken it on board. You will dance and learn.

## IN CONCERT
### Nina Simone, 1964

You've got to learn to leave the table
When love's no longer being served.
—Nina Simone

"The High Priestess of Soul" was her moniker. Classical musician, church singer, jazz vocalist, activist, shit-disturber, intimate of black writers James Baldwin, Lorraine Hansberry, and Langston Hughes, international star, schizophrenic, shouter at audiences, and wild diva, she has a street in Holland named for her. Covered by loads of artists, imitated by none. Nina Simone was a child prodigy who played in church and refused to play until her parents were seated down front with the white people. She was determined to be the first black Woman classical artist. Having been accepted to Juilliard, she was denied entrance to the Curtis Institute in Philadelphia on what she felt was the basis of her race. After the bombing of an Alabama church by the Klan that killed four black girls, and the assassination of civil rights activist Medgar Evers, she wrote "Mississippi

Goddam" as a reaction to the ongoing struggle for equal rights. It is a scathing piece, a from-the-heart lament on the state of race in the USA. In the middle of the song, she says, "This is a show tune, but the show hasn't been written for it yet." Nina Simone lost money to record companies, shot at noisy neighbors, advocated violent revolution, went through bad marriages, had a hit record from a Chanel No. 5 commercial, and all the while was a singular presence and unique voice. Dig her and reach a higher state.

# ART I WISH I HAD
# THE BALLS TO STEAL

First off, the *Mona Lisa* is not on the list. Once you see it, you really can't get over how dinky it is. At least we get to view it, under plastic, with a zillion other people. No one got the chance to have her and view her in Da Vinci's lifetime. Leonardo held tightly on to it. He then gave it to the king of France as a gift when he moved  there in his old age. So France has it for keeps. Meanwhile, centuries later, back at the Louvre, Vincenzo Peruggia, a worker there, just up and snitched it. He simply walked into the gallery, took it off the wall, went into the stairwell, took it out of its frame and case, tucked it under his smock, and walked out with it. Two years later he tried to sell it to an antiques dealer in Florence, Italy, for half a million lire. The dealer, one Mr. Geri, caught on quick, and Peruggia was nabbed. Peruggia claimed Napoleon had stolen the *Mona Lisa* and he wanted it back in Italy, not in France. The painting toured Italy after the cops got it back, and our Vincenzo got only seven months for being a patriotic art thief. Notwithstanding the fact that Napoleon hadn't actually stolen it. It had been in France for hundreds of years as the property of the French Crown. The moral is this: stealing is bad, and art theft is a terrible crime. Don't do it. Let's just pretend. First rule of Proops Art Theft Club: Pretend big or go home.

# A SUNDAY AFTERNOON ON THE ISLAND
# OF LA GRANDE JATTE
## Georges Seurat, created 1884–1886
## (Art Institute of Chicago)

Georges Seurat painted *A Sunday Afternoon* for two years, and then went back and added a border to work with his white frame. There is a monkey on a leash and a Woman fishing, which may be an allusion to the fact people picked up prostitutes on the island. It is an absorbing and active painting, changing texture and color depending on where one stands. It is of course made up of thousands of dots of paint, the technique that would be called pointillism. Seurat died quite young at thirty-one. This burglary would be most tricky, as the piece is almost seven feet tall and ten feet wide. It is as big as a movie screen smack dab in the Art Institute of Chicago. It is also upstairs. We'd have to move at night by tempting the guards with drugged brownies. Then we'd lift the painting frame and all (Seurat designed the frame as well, need that), and march our asses down Michigan Avenue pretending we are a performance art project. Then we jump in the van we have signaled by flashlight. Chance of success: less than 5 percent.

# THE CHICAGO PANELS
## Ellsworth Kelly, created 1989–1999
## (Art Institute of Chicago)

Ellsworth Kelly worked with a camouflage unit during WWII and eventually became an abstract painter and sculptor; he works in shapes and monochromatic canvas. He is a brilliant colorist, and this orange rectangle—one of a series—is in a hallway just at the top of a staircase. It would go perfectly in a home, say, like mine. Right near the fireplace and above my faux-tiger rug just to the right of my thimble collection. We pretend to choke on a souvenir magnet while you grab this canvas and go arse over teakettle out the back. Confederates would be waiting in a black Escalade and off we go. Down to the South Side, where we know a dude to do the deal, then some sinful duck fat fries and a red-hot Chicago-style with a dill pickle spear. We earned it. Chance of success: like the Cubs winning the World Series three times in a row.

## THE ROSE
### Jay Defeo, created 1958–1966
### (Whitney Museum of American Art, New York)

*The Rose* is an impressively unwieldy work of art. It spent years hidden in the San Francisco Art Institute because there was no space massive enough to put the bugger. Twelve feet by nine feet, eight inches thick in places. Covered in jillions of gallons of lead-based paint. *The Rose* weighs over a ton. It took Ms. DeFeo close to eight lengthy, drinking, chain-smoking years to finish and had to be hoisted out of her flat in San Francisco with a forklift. The paint probably contributed to Ms. DeFeo's early shuffling off. It lives now in the Whitney Museum in New York. We'd meet in the cute restaurant, which does brunch. Bloody Marys for nerve, then slowly using our spoons, we'd dig a tunnel under the wall that holds *The Rose* until we undermine the foundation. The weight of the piece will force it to fall onto a bunch of air mattresses we have placed there. This whole plot will take about seventeen years to hatch, so we must guard against impatience. We also need a great big wall to hang it on, so make some inquiries. Chance of success: as small as this work is epic.

# TRIUMPHAL QUADRIGA
## Creator and creation unknown
## (Cathedral at St. Mark's Basilica, Venice)

Everyone who visits Venice goes to St. Mark's and gazes at the magical cathedral. On top are four bronze horses stamping, rearing, majestic. The horses used to live in the Hippodrome in Constantinople. That means they decorated the ancient racetrack in Istanbul. Cast during the Roman Empire, they stood until the Venetians who got to Constantinople in the Fourth Crusade saw them and just *had* to have them. Enrico Dandolo, the blind, ninety-some-odd-years-old doge (Venetians called their leader a doge, pronounced *doje*), led the sack of Constantinople personally as well as arranged for Venice to fund and supply the whole giant undertaking. Everyone ended up in debt to Venice, and Venice ended up with a good chunk of the Byzantine Empire, which was never again quite as strong. Our ancient, crafty, art thief doge sent the horses back, and they were placed on top of St. Mark's. Napoleon stole them when he got there and stuck them on top of his triumphal arch; they got given back after he was exiled. Pollution was wasting them, so they were taken down for their own good, and now they stamp and brood inside the church. We would have to distract everyone with a diversion. You'd go in front and yell, "Chocolate." In the massive confusion of why someone would holler "Chocolate," we'd move in. The horses are simply too huge to move. This is one time art steals us and we are forced to live in situ. *Que sera* and *lasciate i bei tempi rotolo*. Let the good times roll. Chance of success: infinitesimal with a hope of miraculous.

## MAMAN
### Louise Bourgeois, created 1999
### (Guggenheim Museum Bilbao, Spain)

Louise Bourgeois worked for over seventy years. She was finally given her due and recognized by the art world in her seventies. Sculptor, educator, LGBT rights activist, feminist, and confessional artist, she was traumatized as a child by her overbearing dad's affair with her English nanny. This giant spider created from bronze, marble, and stainless steel stands over thirty feet tall with a huge sac of marble eggs. It symbolizes her mother, who died when Louise was twenty-one. This did not go down well with Louise, and she tried to drown herself and was saved by the very same father. *Maman* is French for "mother," and she felt her mother was helpful and protective and could spin and nest. We'd slide into Bilbao like any other tourists, save we have arrived in a crane marked Art Helpers. We would pull up in front of the Guggenheim during siesta and gently lift the spider and slowly drive away into the surrounding mountains. When they awake, it will take some time for them to notice the giant empty space where once clambered a titan-sized arachnid. The Basques celebrate us and create a sexy new rice dish in our honor. After the festivities, we feel guilty and return the ginormous statue the next day. Nothing screams guilt like a symbolic Mother/Spider. It casts its own web of remorse. Chance of success: physically slight, but emotionally we need this.

## LA RÊVE
### Pablo Picasso, created 1932
### (House of Cohen, Connecticut)

Picasso was a pervy fortysomething when he started an affair with seventeen-year-old Marie-Thérèse Walter. She is the subject of this Fauvist piece; its title translates as *The Dream*, which he knocked off in one day. Picasso of course dropped Walter for the photographer and poet Dora Maar. The old swine actually watched them fight it out for him and thought it was one of the best moments of his life. Some artists, huh? It initially went for $4,000, but time and greed pushed the price to the heavens. Steve Wynn is one of those Vegas tycoon types, a billionaire whose understanding of class is to have a dancing waters fountain in front of his hotel that giant bison people from cornfed places ooh and aah at. He bought a gajillion dollars' worth of art a while back: Turner, Picasso, etc. He snorfed up *La Rêve* and put it in a fancy-schmancy gallery in his hotel, which closed due to lack of slot machines and sex workers in the viewing area. One fine, starry, idiotic-rich-people night, while showing the painting off to his famous Hollywood-type friends, Mr. Wynn stuck his elbow through *La Rêve*. This was blamed on his lack of peripheral vision, not to mention lack of supervision. He had agreed the day before to sell it to hedge fund manager and renowned felon Steven A. Cohen for $139 million. Now he owned a torn Picasso of his own making. Something Dalí might have smirked at. He had the painting repaired and sued his insurance company for the price it was devalued at after he clotheslined it. They settled out of court, and Mr. Cohen ended up buying the painting for $155 million. Then Mr. Cohen had to pay the government a billion-dollar fine for being a crooked hedge fund hog, so there is a happy ending. Once this painting hung in a casino, now in a criminal banker's house. Doesn't this work of art deserve to hang somewhere less shady? Say, your house. We'd dress as pizza delivery professionals and when we are inevitably shown to the servants' entrance, you run in and grab it off the wall and put it in the pizza box while sparklers are lit to sidetrack the domestics. We would all go global with this heist, so be prepared to sell this to a middleman of low repute and dwell in Belize under an assumed name for at least fifteen years. We'd go by Mr. Van Deterich and assume a limp and a slight Dutch accent. Since Dutch is a difficult accent, a slight one will serve. Chance of success: realistic. If the non-gifted can be rich and stupid, why can't we?

## THE LESHAN GIANT BUDDHA
### Haitong and disciples, created 713–803
### (Leshan, Sichuan Province)

The Leshan Giant Buddha is enormous, towering over the confluence of the Minjiang, Dadu, and Qingyi Rivers in China's Sichuan province. A monk named Haitong started this colossal project in 713. He ran out of money and apparently pulled his eyes out in grief. Funding came back, and it was finished some seventy years later. This sitting Buddha is 233 feet tall, and you can perch on its little toenail with loads of room for friends. The mountain above has spectacular sunsets and clouds sailing all around like a dream. There are also loads of feisty and mischevious macaques running about, the red-faced monkeys that are so often used by people as test animals. They are rife with herpes, which they don't suffer from. But they do not make good pets, so do not touch or otherwise accost them. The Leshan Buddha is far too big to steal, so we will have to work quickly with mirrors. The place is heaving with pilgrims and tourists and assuredly phalanxes of Red Army as well. You shine the reflected sun in their eyes, and we will hypnotize everyone instantly using opiated incense. Then when they are lulled, we change the course of the river and just float on by. But wait. Better yet, let's just make this a Zen theft: we see the Buddha, we want to possess the Buddha, we come to the realization that we cannot attain the Buddha, we have been dishonest with ourselves. We let it go and go get Chinese food. Chance of success: as good as anything in the universe has.

## EL MUNDO MÁGICO DE LOS MAYAS
Leonora Carrington, created 1965–1966
(Museo Nacional de Antropología, Mexico City)

Leonora Carrington was a painter as well as a spiritualist, sculptor, novelist, historian, and sometime alchemist. Born into a wealthy family in England, she moved to Europe and joined the Surrealist movement. She had an affair with the famous German artist Max Ernst, but she lost him to rich art patron and full-time artist chaser Peggy Guggenheim. This did not help her mental state. She broke down and was given horrible drugs and electroshock therapy. But she managed to come out on the other side and escaped from the mental hospital. She then wrote a novel about her experience, *Down Below*, and moved to Mexico where she spent a good deal of the rest of her long ninety-four-year life. What was it about Women artists of that generation? Louise Bourgeois lived to be ninety-eight, Agnes Martin to ninety-two. Anyway, they dug her in Mexico, and she had many shows and was considered a Mexican artist. She was given a commission to do a mural about the pre-white-people history of Mexico and went to Chiapas to study the area. She was introduced by the anthropologist Gertrude Blom to the *curanderos*, or healers, from the awesomely named town of Zinacantán (the land of bats). They normally didn't do their thing for outsiders, but Ms. Carrington had such a vast knowledge and respect for mysticism and healing, they let her sit in. She studied the Popol Vuh, or people's history, which is the Mayan sacred book of mysteries before the conquistadors. From this time she painted *The Magical World of the Mayas*. This painting resides in Chapultepec Park in Mexico City, so we should take a shamanistic dose of psychoactive mushrooms that we have bought from a lady named Carmelita we met in a bodega. You get too high and start to freak, so we stop for *refrescos* at a stand. The afternoon is still and we can hear children playing, so your sense of dread abates somewhat, and we sally to the museum. There in the warm glow of altered perception, we become overwhelmed by the astounding colors and fantastical motif. Imbued with a sense of belonging to the universe, we abandon our notion of physical theft and decide to have an unlikely escapade in a brightly colored cab. Later, when we are coming down, we have seafood enchiladas and revel in our refound sense of cosmic morality. So goes the flow. Chance of success: mythical, like the Lizard God returning.

## THE SCREAM
### Edvard Munch, created 1893–1910
### (Munch Museum and The National Gallery, Oslo)

Why not? Everyone else has stolen it. There are five *Screams*, and they have been taken time and time again. They were heisted in the recent past, and the thieves wrote a note saying thanks for the bad security. Everyone is incarcerated now, but *The Scream* is waiting for another larcenous visit. This time we'd do it right. We all go in and scream in abject existential terror, and while the staff puzzles this out, we run for the snack bar where—we kid thou not—there are *Scream*-themed cakes. A *Scream* cake fight is started, and in the ensuing kerfuffle, we back our tourist bus up to the front entrance and roll on down the hill. A waiting boat on the fjord takes us to one of a million little islands where we sit drinking aquavit and ponder why we just did that. Munch would approve, as he was a depressive drunk. Who else would experience a lovely summer sunset on a bridge as a moment of wailing futility? Chance of success: actually better than any other plan.

## DAVID
### Donatello, created 1430–1440
### (Museo Nazionale del Bargello, Florence)

Florence is bursting with fabulous art, including Michelangelo's *David*, Botticelli's *The Birth of Venus*, and of course Brunelleschi's astounding Duomo. All too obvious and well guarded. The line alone at the Uffizi will kill any urge to view art, much less purloin. Then why Donatello's *David*? For one thing, it is small compared to the other *David*. Just around five feet tall. Michelangelo made his hero boy fifteen feet tall. Plus there is a full-sized plaster cast in the V&A in London and a full-sized marble in the Royal Botanic Gardens in Surrey. So they have backups.

Donatello's *David* stands in perfect *contrapposto*, which Donatello certainly learned from looking at ancient Greek and Roman sculpture. That means he looks like a Woman and has his sassy hand on his hip. He wears a small helmet and has a giant sword that represents exactly what you think it does. We make small talk with the guards about the weather and the price of designer leather goods. Then two drunken colleagues enter with a nude man wearing a helmet. We knock David off his pedestal, and the drunks hurry him out on either side with a loud excuse: "He's always like this after lunch, doesn't know his limit." The sight of the nude man in a hat with a sword should be enough for us to make our escape in a late-'90s model Fiat Punto. Then it's off to a secluded crib in Tuscany for Chianti and goose prosciutto. Chances of success: slim and biblical, like our hero.

## ELGIN MARBLES
### Phidias, created c. 447–438 BC
### (British Museum, London)

Lord Elgin, who was ambassador to the Ottoman Empire, nicked the marbles—meaning statues and reliefs of heroic heroes being heroic—from the Parthenon and other temples in Greece. The Turks had been running Greece for 350 years. Elgin thought the Turks were wrecking the art and sculpture and received permission from the government to start lifting them. On the way, some sank in a boat and had to be recovered. Was it a curse? Greece has been petitioning to get them back for a long while. The British Museum refuses to part with them. Time for us to get them back for Greece. This one we don't do for gain but for immortality. The British Museum website states they were "acquired," which means pilfered. The museum bought them from Elgin after much ado, and they low-balled him on the price. We'd come disguised as a moving company and say we are taking the statues out for a wash. We'd load up the van and speed to the coast, where we have hired a Greek vessel with a ne'er-do-well captain named Stavros. We would then sail back the same route the marbles came, and when we hit Greece, we'd alert the New Acropolis Museum, where they already have a room prepared for the treasures awaiting their return. We'd dine in triumph; you get the mullet, and I get the lamb. We'd send the plaster casts back to the British Museum with a note saying the cleaning was free. Chance of success: hang the success; we did this for the gods.

## PAINTINGS
### George W. Bush, created c. 2010
### (Dick Cheney's Fridge, Wyoming)

George W. Bush was almost voted president twice during the ter-ror/war/depression boom of the 2000s. Dick Cheney was nomi-nally vice president, but in reality he was the shot caller. Since his retirement from public life, W has been pursuing his goal of being the worst artist who ever held office since Hitler. His portraits of world leaders he has met are a tribute to the primitive school of *art brut,* or outsider art, usually meaning art made by people from without the art world, such as children or mental patients. Cheney's house in Wyoming is filled with trophies and war crime memorabilia. We'd pitch up as an honor guard with a band, uni-forms, and everything. We would perform a number on the lawn and ask to use the facilities. On our way to the loo, we'd steal the Putin portrait off the refrigerator and drive like fury. We can be at the Devil's Tower (non-ironic) before noon and then, freedom. Win/win. Chance of success: like winning a war in Afghanistan.

# VODKA-FLAVORED VODKA

I live on shameless flattery . . . and vodka . . .
but the two usually go hand in hand.
—Vicktor Alexander

Vodka fell from heaven at the gods' caprice. A cold, clear, bracing
shower. The one that saved humankind from itself. The planets
had spun too far away, the forces of good were abating. Vodka
descended and chilled the Earth so we could survive in this caustic, poetry-barren atmosphere.

Beautiful, benign, multihued bubbles rose from the puddles
of the new ambrosia. Exploding in effervescent flashes that salve
the soul and delight the winkles of your cockle. Like an unsullied
lake from a zillion-page Russian novel, vodka lies waiting for you
to dare. *Vodka* means "water" in many languages. Water is simply
vodka reduced to survival mode. Water is vodka that won't fight,
merely survive. Liquid inspiration, crystal-clear nectar, the monarch of spirits, breakfast of champions, companion to caviar and
sassy radishes, bloodier of Marys, emergency antiseptic, handler of
Chelsea. Take it not lightly, but do take it nightly. Vodka is a boon
friend that never lets you down. Scientists assert vodka is a depressant. Fuck that. Watching the Learning Channel is a depressant;
vodka takes us where we need to be, to the mellow, altered state

of bliss just over the border from where you were when your boss climbed up your ass like an armadillo. People ask, "What kind is your favorite?" The answer is, "Do it come in a bottle?" Beware the flavored kinds. Vodka already has a flavor—it is its flavor. You don't need fruity kiddie-flavored vodka any more than you need vodka-flavored fruity vodka drinks. Fruit joins vodka; it should not blag its way in and perform cold fusion with the flaves. No one in Russia or Poland or Finland drinks vodka with fizzy soda pop while watching crappy sports in a loud bar. They drink it freezing cold gathered in secret, sullen reading groups. They know it is too profound a drink to besmirch in that way. Never mix; never feel disappointment.

### *The Smartest Book in the World* VODKA RECIPES

#### *Vodka-Flavored Vodka Drink*

1 bottle of vodka
1 bucket of ice
1 bowl of lemons (sliced)
1 glass (any size will do but something short of a flagon)
1 moon
1 vast field of stars

Fill glass with ice. Add lemon. Pour a heaping tot. Silence any heaping tots in the vicinity. Gaze skyward at the moon. Add stars. Listen to the music of the spheres. Drain glass. Refill. Consider your life. Consider changing it. Reload. When the bottle is empty, you will have come to a decision. Seize the day.

### Vodka Goddess Swirling

1 bottle of vodka
1 bucket of ice
1 bowl of lemons (wedged)
1 glass, shot-sized
1 tumbler
1 telephone

Chill bottle in freezer. Take bottle from freezer. Promptly fill shot glass with vodka. Drink immediately. Fill tumbler with ice. Add lemon wedge. Fill with vodka. Drink with relaxed, rocking motion. Alternate between shots and tumblers. Dance. Call old friend. Cry tears of joy. Compose a letter of thanks on that stationery you have been saving.

### Vodka-Flavored Funky Screwdriver

1 bottle of vodka
1 bucket of ice
1 bowl of lemons (sliced)
4 glasses
1 jam kicker with which to kick jams

Take four glasses and fill to the brim with ice. Add a slice of lemon to each. Offer the following toast: "May we never be farther apart" or "Let's do this, kittens." Turn on jam kicker. Play funk jams. Let the funk preside. Repeat. Rest. Switch jam kicker to "The Smartest Man in the World" podcast. Listen. Feel renewed. Wipe tears of unalterable joy from face. Return to funk.

## Proople Rain

1 bottle of vodka
1 bucket of ice
1 bowl of lemons (sliced)
1 glass

Fill glass with ice. Add lemon. Pour vodka to brim. Guzzle gently. Lean on wall. Sing show tunes. Make up your mind to quit your job and become a freelance sex symbol. Or Argentinian rancher. Or expert on Asian art. Or mystery millionaire philanthropist. Stir. Renew. Repeat if ambulatory.

# NOTES, ADDENDUM, ERRATA, AND ERIK ESTRADA

Firstly, a note on the Oxford comma. It is employed throughout the book. This was specifically against my wishes; I was sentenced by the publishers to sit captive in a darkened room with ghastly, uncomfortable furnishings, horrible music by Sting, and dismal New York weed while they peppered my masterpiece with this abomination of punctuation. The willful disregard for my feelings on this matter is an illustrative example of how the sincere common person is being trod upon by the vast, unsympathetic corporate powers that be. This explanation is the one that I prefer to believe rather than the fact that I never perused my copy of *The Elements of Style* by Strunk and White. I instead used it to balance a wonky table leg. There, I feel it finally served some purpose. The Oxford comma and I have called a truce. The exclamation point had better watch out if I see its overenthusiastic lame ass in a dark alley.

As for the amount of poetry in the book, medicine does not always taste good, but it can make you well. I am not certain what that means. At the outset, it seemed a good idea to shove some old-fashioned culture in here. I may possum have been misapprehending. There is a boatload of poetry and baseball. I don't apologize; I merely note and agree with you that it was a lot. Try reading the poetry aloud—even better, have someone read it aloud to you while you lie recumbent on velvet cushions drinking cherry wine and smoking a hookah. That ought to solve any metric problems. For the next book, if there is one, less baseball and more Women athletes, scientists, artists, and heroes. This I vow to Diana.

Books form the major source of information in this tome. We stayed away from wiki anything for obvious reasons. My vast personal experience as a groom, paperboy, pizza delivery dude, steelworker, longshoreman, rodeo clown, baseball fan, comic, waitress, busboy, improvateur, car parker, kitten wrangler, voice-over artist, world traveler, and amateur drug addict also informed my writing. For your information, darling, this book was extensively fact-checked by one Ms. Tate, who was meticulous and quite helpful, arguing every morsel down to where Satchel Paige met his first wife and which baseball executive proclaimed Japanese players would never play in the big leagues. That was not from a book but an actual question I posed to an executive in the press box at the San Francisco Giants spring-training facility in 1987. I asked if he thought we would ever have Japanese players in the bigs and he responded to me, "Never." I responded, "That is what they said about blacks during World War II." His beardy mug darkened and he scowled at me, not happy with my youthful brash attitude and being called out on his wholesale racism, but *sic semper tyrannis*. I was there literally on a pass. *Ex ore infantium.* As for Paige, there is no one figure on whom you may rely on less to tell the whole truth. John Holway, acclaimed historian of the Negro Leagues, starts his book *Voices from the Great Black Baseball Leagues* with this quote from Napoleon: "History is a myth agreed upon." Then let us agree.

Speaking of myth, there is a comprehensive book on Casey at the Bat in all of its permutations and implications called *Mighty Casey: All American* by Eugene C. Murdock, 1984.

More baseball books have I consumed than you have had hot meals. This we presume is not a surprise to you, dear reader. We will not list them all but hit you with some highlights. Donald Hall's *Fathers Playing Catch with Sons* has terrific first-person material with colorful pitcher Dock Ellis. Indeed, Mr. Hall wrote a biography with Dock called *Dock Ellis in the Country of Baseball*. Hall is a poet as well as a very good writer and journalist, so I find his writing far more entertaining than the usual baseball history. He cares. Well, almost all baseball authors care because they are sick with it. Leigh Montville authored *The Big Bam: The Life and Times of Babe Ruth* and *Ted Williams: The Biography of an American Hero*, both so groovy you don't have to like baseball to dig them. Robert Creamer is a distinguished baseball writer with loads of sensational biographies where he gets to the core of the player—*Babe: The Legend Comes to Life* and *Stengel: His Life and Times* are where you should start if you want the real story. My favorite book about old-time ball is *The Glory of Their Times* by Larry Ritter. He personally interviewed dozens of pre-WWI players, and you can download the actual recordings. To hear the old men speak of hanging out at firehouses and finding hairpins for good luck . . . It is not mere nostalgia, it is great oral history. I had the fortune of meeting and hanging with Larry Ritter, and he was one of nature's gentlemen. An unusual book about Ruth that astounded me with stories I had never known is *The Year Babe Ruth Hit 104 Home Runs* by Bill Jenkinson. It shows Ruth to be a superhuman baller. Other great baseball authors whose work I consulted include: the amazingly informed Donald Honig; the magisterial Dr. Harold Seymour; John Thorn, who appears to know everything about the game—maybe because he is the game's official historian; and Charles Alexander's biographies of Ty Cobb and John McGraw, which are vivid and frank. Also Cait Murphy, who wrote a wild ride called *Crazy '08: How a Cast of Cranks, Rogues, Boneheads, and Magnates Created the Greatest Year in Baseball History*. And Jane Leavy wrote the warts-and-all biography *The Last Boy: Mickey Mantle and the End of America's Childhood*. Hank Aaron wrote his own book, *I Had a Hammer*, which is characteristically honest about his life and the racism he endured.

Willie Mays is my favorite player and I have read a bunch of books about him. I read all the kiddie ones when I was little, which are still fun if you can find them. For now, the definitive authorized biography *Willie Mays: The Life, the Legend* by James S. Hirsch is the standard, but *Say Hey: The Autobiography of Willie Mays* by Mays with Lou Sahadi and *Willie's Time* and *Willie Mays: My Life In and Out of Baseball* by Charles Einstein are far more fun and anecdotal. Einstein also edited the awesome Fireside Book of Baseball series and was the son of vaudeville comic Harry Einstein and the half-brother of comedians Super Dave Osborne and Albert Brooks. So there. Start there, oh novice baseball reader. If you have the grit.

The Negro Leagues and Satchel Paige have been covered wonderfully by many better scribes than I. The ball got rolling in 1970 with Robert Peterson's *Only the Ball Was White.* Much has been done about writing the history of the Negro Leagues since that book came out, but no one had ever bothered to get the story from the players' mouths, so now everyone follows in Peterson's wake. *Baseball's Great Experiment* by Jules Tygiel is a riveting account not only of Jackie Robinson but also of the frustration that many veteran Negro League players felt over being shuttled about in the minor leagues. It is also candid about the white owners and press. Jackie Robinson wrote many books and I have sourced from them all. *I Never Had It Made,* his autobiography with Alfred Duckett, is tremendously gripping. *Baseball Has Done It* is Jackie Robinson's take on the game after he left. The new version was reprinted in 2005 and has a very informative preface by Spike Lee. *Opening Day* by Jonathan Eig was given to me by my editor, Matthew Benjamin, and is a terrific and informative book about Jackie's first season. Satchel Paige was, among many things, an author, and his two autobiographies, *Maybe I'll Pitch Forever* with John Holway and David Lipman and *Pitchin' Man* with Hal Lebovitz, are truly delightful and painful. Larry Tye wrote the recent Satchel biography *Satchel: The Life and Times of an American Legend*, and it is well worth it. Beautifully researched. But my favorite book on

Paige is William Price Fox's *Satchel Paige's America*. It starts with Fox meeting Paige in the Twilight Zone Lounge at the Rhythm Lanes bowling alley in Kansas City, where he is drinking beer, smoking, and holding court. They spend a week together, and Paige takes him out for barbecue, to a nightclub, to get a new muffler, and to play ball with a kids' team he is putting together. Paige is a hero and a celebrity everywhere they go, and he teaches Fox about growing up in Alabama, and how to hunt, fish, cook a burger, do a cakewalk, and live your life like a legend. Amazing, moving, human book, and quite short. *A Complete History of the Negro Leagues 1884-1955* by Mark Ribowsky is quietly factual and a great resource. For my money, the greatest authority on the Negro Leagues is John Holway. He went to his first Negro League game in 1945 and saw Paige's Monarchs play Josh Gibson's Homestead Grays. His first-person interviews with all the living Negro League players are the most entertaining and enlightening books on the subject. *Black Diamonds: Life in the Negro Leagues from the Men Who Lived It*, *Voices from the Great Black Baseball Leagues*, and *Black Ball Stars* have interviews with Cool Papa Bell, Willie Wells, and Effa Manley, the Woman owner of the Newark Eagles. I also consulted Holway's *Josh Gibson* and *Josh and Satch*.

Ancient history is best told by the ancients, all of whom had an agenda, and from the distant past you can hear the distinct sound of axes grinding. Suetonius' *The Twelve Caesars* is rude, ribald, partially factual when he could be bothered, and also just great reading. He covers the first twelve emperors, and that includes Caligula and Nero, so dig in. *Julius Caesar* by Nigel Cawthorne is a splendid little book that hits all the high points. Perfect if you just want to while away an afternoon with lust and carnage. Dr. Adrian Goldsworthy has written on Caesar and Cleopatra and Antony. He can be a bit straightforward, which is no crime, but the work is fascinating. I found his *Caesar: Life of a Colossus* and *Antony and Cleopatra* to be most helpful. Honestly, I quite enjoyed the bestseller *Cleopatra: A Life* by Stacy Schiff. Anyone who can fling the phrase "cool raspberry dawns" into a history book has me by the asp.

Among the many books on Alexander the Great, some are painfully detailed and others whole cloth. Plutarch wrote *Parallel Lives* and used Julius Caesar and Alexander as his conquerors. Plutarch is great fun, and he certainly twists the story to suit his own needs, sometimes forcing the analogy between the two generals. He prefers illustrative tales to dates and facts. Don't we all? Arrian's *Anabasis of Alexander* clips along, and he is sometimes judgmental about our hero. All to the good. Arrian was well educated, lifelong pals with Roman Emperor Hadrian, wrote loads of books, and had a huge career in Roman politics, holding many posts. He sources Ptolemy, who was Alexander's close friend and general, as well as Nearchus, an admiral of the fleet. Robin Lane Fox is a historian and an expert gardener; his *Alexander the Great* is a beautifully realized portrait and one I would highly suggest if you are questing for more. I also found his engaging portrait of ancient times, *The Classical World: An Epic History from Homer to Hadrian*, a great way to get an overview if that is what you seek. Lewis V. Cummings was a cartographer for the British Intelligence Service, and his *Alexander the Great* is exhaustive and detailed and wow, strap in for maps and places and dates, but he has the best account of Alexander at Malia, fighting for his life. Skip it unless you want to go deep. *Alexander the Great* by Professor Norman F. Cantor is a lovely and personal tale. Notice how all the books have the same title? I guess so you don't get dazzled by other less great Alexanders.

Will and Ariel Durant are the great humanists of historians. They always emphasize the role of the powerful over the weak. We used Volumes 2 (*The Life of Greece*) and 3 (*Caesar and Christ*) of their gigantic eleven-volume *The Story of Civilization* for the chapters on Alexander and Julius Caesar.

As for general history, *Lies My Teacher Told Me* by James W. Loewen is a blinders-off look at American "history." The kind we were fed because it sounded better than the truth. Of course, *A People's History of the United States* by Howard Zinn will set you straight on what really happened to the poor and disenfranchised, and will have you marching in the streets with a picket sign in a minute. The singer, author, and educator Gil Scott-Heron has a revealing biography called *The Last Holiday* that takes you way past the music and has great asides, such as that Bob Marley was kind of a knob sometimes. Flashy feminist bad-ass Florynce Kennedy wrote a biography that has her wearing a cowboy hat and flipping the bird on the cover called *Color Me Flo: My Hard Life and Good Times.* Similar to Ms. Kennedy herself, it is hard to beat for honesty about race and sex in America. *Passing It On* by Yuri Kochiyama is a memoir of a life-long activist and a warning against complacency.

Movies are quite personal. One individual's *Godfather* is another person's *Coyote Ugly.* A lifetime of being a fan is all I can plead. I was the movie critic for my high school paper. It was the mid-'70s and a great time for pictures, and I remember reviewing *Young Frankenstein* and *The Three Musketeers* and having a huge crush on Faye Dunaway and Cybill Shepherd.

Most of the films in this book have been shown at The Greg Proops Film Club, which is a monthly happening at Cinefamily in fabulous Hollywood in the gracious overpriced athletic-shoe district.

*Easy Riders, Raging Bulls* by Peter Biskind is the funnest kind of film book, druggy and gossipy with lots of references to great movies like *Chinatown* and *Mean Streets.* Can you discuss film without Pauline Kael? Her *For Keeps: 30 Years at the Movies* is one million pages and worth it for the fights you will have with her in your head. *Making Movies* by Sidney Lumet is how he did it in a book. Perfect for intermission.

Jennifer Canaga, the illustrator and my erstwhile child bride, has hipped me to most of the literature and movies and artwork found in this book. We came up with the idea of stealing art while at the Musée Marmottan Monet. The car park is located right below and it would have been nothing to pitch a priceless painting out the window while I pretended to have a seizure and our confederates stole away into the Parisian night. Alas, we stayed on the narrow. Jennifer has of course changed my outlook on life, and this book would never have happened without her support. She was the one who convinced me to do a podcast, and she is actually well read. As opposed to my glib horizontal knowledge of junk and stuff and things no one likes.

Erik Estrada is still handsome and lives in Hollywood Hills.

# ACKNOWLEDGMENTS

The *Smartest Book* wishes to thank the following people for getting this thing done:

Jennifer Canaga, my beloved wife, collaborator, and illustrator of this book. She does the research, plants the ideas, and anything cool is her doing. You are the Smartest Woman in the World. You are the reason. Eternally.

David Tochterman, the man who made this happen.

Matthew Benjamin, who drove me like a chariot. You are a mensch.

Elaine Wilson, who had to read this more than anyone.

Matt Belknap, for convincing me to do the podcast. You were right.

Ryan McManemin, for convincing me to do the podcast. You were right as well.

Lee Kernis, for managing.

Bob Voice and Nicola Hobbs, for always believing.

Hadrian Belove and Bret Berg at Cinefamily, for encouraging us to show pictures for the Greg Proops Film Club.

Troy Conrad, for being so cool and caring.

Andrew Strapp, for his generosity.

Linda Sawicki, for her perseverance.

Thanks for the love, way love you back: Ryan Stiles, Drew Carey, Doug Benson, Phil Beauman, Chris Hardwick, Nick Franglen, Tom Sawyer, Will and Debi Durst, Warren Thomas, Lauretta Feldman, Paul Provenza, Justin Edbrooke, Rich Super, Joe Rogan, Molly Schminke, Adam Carolla, Jay Mohr, Jessica Herman-Weitz, Jen Kirkman, Greg Fitzsimmons, Kevin Pollack, Jackie Kashian, Allison Rosen, Jeff Davis, Jimmy Dore, David

Feldman, Ric Overton, Nick Jones, Alex Gaylon, Scott McGee, Dan Patterson, Tom Fineman, and Mark Leveson.

All the lovely kittens who have come to and listened to my podcast and given me more than I will ever be able to thank you for, you mean the world to me.

Kittens McTavish, I don't need you. Thanks, but.

May every Paige you turn be a Satchel Paige, may every Bell that rings be a Cool Papa Bell, and if you must buy bonds, make sure they are Barry Bonds.

# INDEX

# ABOUT THE AUTHOR

Greg Proops is a stand-up comic from San Francisco, best known for his unpredictable appearances on *Whose Line Is It Anyway?* Mr. Proops records the chart-topping and much-celebrated "The Smartest Man in the World" podcast live from around the world and, somehow, Cleveland. Mr. Proops has also been a voice actor in *Star Wars: Episode I—The Phantom Menace* and was Bob in *Bob the Builder*. He lives in Hollywood. It's not that bad, really. You can find him at Gregproops.com.